# *L.A.*

L.A.

July 21, 1983

Robert miles
Parker E

VIEW
FROM
WELCOME
STREET

# L.A.

## ROBERT MILES PARKER

HARCOURT BRACE JOVANOVICH, PUBLISHERS

SAN DIEGO    NEW YORK    LONDON

**HBJ**

Requests for permission to make copies of any part of the work should be mailed to:
Permissions, Harcourt Brace Jovanovich, Publishers, Orlando, Florida 32887.

Library of Congress Cataloging in Publication Data
Parker, Robert Miles.
   L.A.
   1. Los Angeles (Calif.)—Buildings.   2. Architecture—
California—Los Angeles.   I. Title.   II. Title: LA.
NA735.L55P37   1984      720'.9794'94      83-26383

ISBN 0-15-147300-5
       0-15-647590-1 (Pbk.)

Designed by Dalia Hartman

Printed in the United States of America

First edition

A B C D E

For Merika

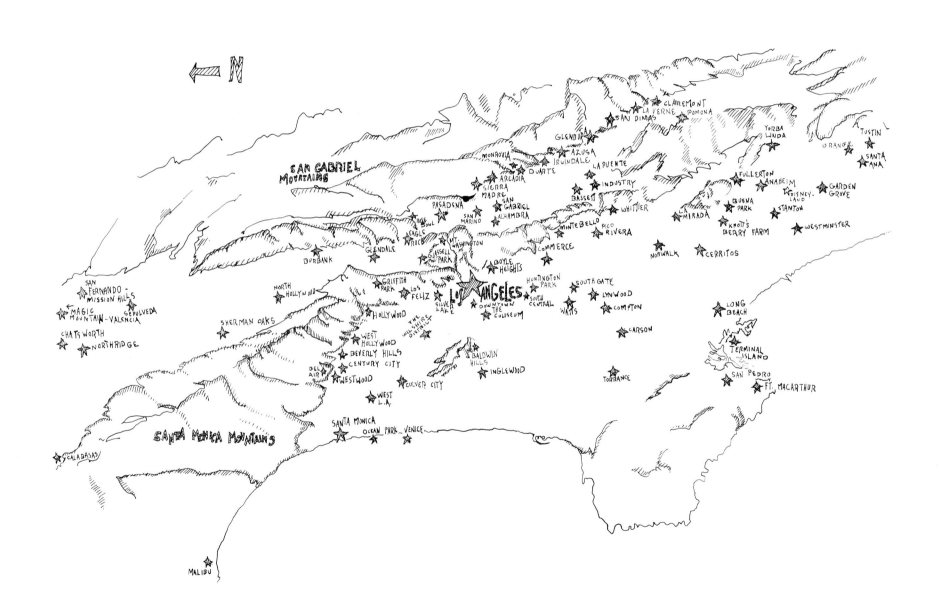

# CONTENTS

# ACKNOWLEDGMENTS

From bag ladies to city officials, hundreds of anonymous people shared their personal Los Angeles with me, each of them leaving a bit of his or her life in the ink lines of my drawings.

Of course, there are plenty of un-anonymous people who helped and guided me throughout this project. I remember Paul McNally in Hollywood, Tom Clausen in Anaheim, and Carol and David Fluke, who traded a week at their Buena Park motel for a drawing. John Chamberlin gave me Park La Brea, Jerry Kaye, the Hollywood Flats. John Wise shared West Hollywood, and Peter Bailey, Glendale and Eagle Rock. Pat Diamond gave me Fullerton, and Peter De Luca, the Wilshire District. Peter Adams shared Pasadena, and the Claremont Colleges gave the Katie dog and me a guest house for my adventures in the San Gabriel Valley.

Two books were also of particular assistance: David Gebhard and Robert Winter's *Guide to Architecture in Los Angeles & Southern California* and Paul Gleye's *The Architecture of Los Angeles*.

Without the guidance of Glenda and Cal Hamilton, Martha and Eddie Alf, Dr. Laud Humphries, and David Cameron, my L.A. experience would have been much less complete. Commander Robin Reighley and the crew of the USS *Berkeley* offered their Los Angeles, and Lt. Colonel Jean Klick shared Fort MacArthur. I especially thank Hilary and Richard Sanderson for making me part of the family. And Terry Horton—thank you for always being there.

On the home front, I want to thank my editor, John Woods, who nagged me endlessly and believed in my dream; Doug Lenhart, my personal secretary/confidant, who listened to my stories about L.A. and helped me refine them; and my assistant, David Lange, who patiently followed all my mad directions. The project could not have been accomplished without them.

# INTRODUCTION

Since I was a boy, I have been amazed by the sheer size and diversity of Los Angeles. The city ranges from the ocean to the mountains, from the near bottomland of Orange County to the almost desert in the north. One neighborhood may be called Alhambra and another Bel Air, but it's all Los Angeles to me.

For the purpose of my formalized exploration, I decided that Los Angeles is any place that thinks it is L.A. Claremont, for instance, sees itself as a unique, intellectual center, yet also as a distant but particular throb of the city's heart. And out in Tustin, too, people are related to downtown—they work there. But places like Newport and Laguna have a different air—they think of themselves as something apart, something beyond; they just don't seem part of the big city.

My way of understanding the city was simply to look at it. With an old director's chair, a drawing board, and, on most occasions, my dog Katie, I would sit and draw. There's an immediacy to my style: I never use a pencil for preliminary work; I just use a pot of ink and an old-fashioned dip pen, and I try to record on the board what I see. What goes down on the board stays there, including the blops, the smears, the raindrops. . . .

I tried to examine all the dozens of independent towns and neighborhoods that make up what I've declared to be greater L.A. Sometimes I found nothing I wanted to draw—that's the reason some well-known places are not included in this collection. And there are places that I just never got to—knowing I could spend my whole life drawing in Los Angeles. But what's here captures a unique place at one moment in its history.

I tried to choose buildings (I love buildings—they're like people, only they keep still) that reflect the particular personality of an area. For instance, the Castle Green in Pasadena really suggests the mad yet sophisticated glory that that city once had and perhaps still has. Sometimes my choices were made at the requests of friends, who then became collectors. Most often, however, buildings would reach out and grab me. The Doria Apartments was one of those. I was weary after a long day of drawing downtown, and it was almost dark—but the Doria jumped up and demanded that I draw some more.

I discovered two rather exotic motifs in Los Angeles architecture. Wherever I went there were shiplike structures. And, more often than not, right around the corner would be something Aztec or Mayan. Look around—those two styles, nautical and Mayan, are everywhere, cheek by jowl. Absurd, you might say. Well, that's Los Angeles. I've never been to another city that boasts deserted night clubs like Mt. Baldy or tamales that you step into for a Mexican snack. Where else does the Coca-Cola Bottling Company resemble an ocean liner? And then there are magic castles, Good Knight Inns, Hobbit houses, and the Venice arcade. Los Angeles continually makes me smile. Even the freeways are okay. Just don't drive during rush hours. And if you do, it's a grand time for looking at buildings.

I'm biased, but in many ways Los Angeles is America's greatest city. It has all the elements of a good story: a romantic past, a glorious present, and an outrageous future ahead. And it's all recorded—L.A.'s architecture is its autobiography. I hope you enjoy the tale.

# THE CITY
# AND
# WESTLAKE

**The Howell Hotel and Art Theatre
550 South Main Street**

Main Street was Los Angeles's burlesque street and was once lined with many early-twentieth-century theaters. Some remnants of that honky-tonk time still stand, reflected in the glint of gutterside bottles.

**View into Downtown** (overleaf)
**Glendale Boulevard and Cortez Street**

Los Angeles is a mix of old and new. Drive almost any street that feeds into downtown, and you will be delighted—from all directions you travel through the history of the city. There are remnants of the 1880s—Victorian Los Angeles. Pieces of mission revival L.A. may jump into view. If you're lucky, you may even see an example of the absurd architecture that L.A. has always been famous for (perhaps a tamale palace or maybe a Mayan temple). Arriving, finally, at the futuresque downtown, you may be bewildered—you'll have seen a surfeit of treasures—but you will want more.

## The Mayan Theatre
## 1044 South Hill

One of the most amazing buildings in all Los Angeles is the Mayan Theatre. It's a mythic structure, lifted out of the jungles of Central America. You feel you may need a machete to chop your way in. The facade of the theater is a crawling collage of Mayan designs. Seven warriors glare down at you. But they're only part of a composition into which are woven hundreds of faces, decorative tiles, and Mayan hieroglyphs.

The Mayan was built in 1927, when excess was de rigueur. Tired of standard styles, architects stole ideas from all over the ancient world. The place might not fit in the Yucatan, but it sure looks good on Hill Street in downtown L.A.

Morgan, Walls, and Clements were the theater's architects, and the sculpture was created by Francisco Comeja. Originally, the facade was gray concrete. It is now absurd and glorious in rainbow hues. The interior is no less wondrous—a dank, almost pungent Mayan tomb. The facade carvings are repeated in water fountains and stairway guards, and they even appear behind the concession stand. Instead of priests and maidens, dirty movies now dance on the great silver screen, vaguely appropriate to the murky gloom.

**The *Herald Examiner* Building**
**1111 South Broadway**

On the lower end of Broadway sits the *Herald Examiner*. Wrapped in a reprise of a California mission, it belongs in the desolate stetches of this desertlike part of downtown.

Commissioned by William Randolph Hearst and created by Julia Morgan (she also designed Hearst's castle at San Simeon), the structure seems to say—"What! They write a newspaper inside of me?" And indeed

they do, a paper that is ofttimes as flashy as its home.

The mission revival style used to evoke sneers from lots of eminent art historians. It is increasingly recognized for what it was and is: a delightful re-examination of Southern California's heritage. There are usually the look of simulated adobe, some scalloped parapets, a bell tower, and an arcade (or at

least one arch). The *Examiner*'s arches, by the way, once held giant windows. They had to be plastered over during labor troubles.

The *Herald Examiner* Building occupies its space proudly as a newspaper should. At the same time it hunkers low, hugging the arid Los Angeles landscape.

**The Bonaventure Hotel** (*below*)
**Fifth and Figueroa**

John Portman's 1976 Bonaventure Hotel is glory stacked above the city streets. Unfortunately, he didn't stack it high enough. Those cylinders should zoom far up into the sometimes blue Los Angeles sky. Instead, they squat on cement foundations. From street level, there is nothing to see but a bunker of stories-high concrete. The street world is not a part of the sleek Bonaventure. Costumed guards greet guests and whisk them from car to lobby in the blink of an eye, rescuing them from the gibbering old men and derelict bag ladies who haunt the sidewalks.

The trees in this view are deceiving—they're growing in a cement garden three stories above the ground. I too was above street level as I drew them, perched in a manicured cement plaza. It's not necessary to become pedestrianized to visit the Bonaventure. From the parking garage you escalate and glide past concrete bastions into the futureworld of the hotel lobby. The interior is a set of interlocking circles, confusing and amusing.

**City Hall** (*above*)
**200 North Spring Street**

Although it was constructed way back in the late twenties (John C. Austin, John Parkinson, Albert C. Martin, and Austin Whittlesey were its architects), the Los Angeles City Hall continues to be the focal point for downtown. Mind you, the new plastic and glass high rises are bigger and more brashly colored, but your eye always travels to the Assyrian tower of City Hall. Its lean twenty-eight stories still demand that there should be clean city government going on inside. When it was built, the style was designated as Italian Classic. Now it's dated but dramatic Deco.

## The Downtown Library (above)
### 630 West Fifth Street

Looking every bit like the leftover it is, the Los Angeles Central Library sits mournfully between glassy modern L.A. and funky old downtown. The library was designed by Bertram G. Goodhue and completed posthumously in 1926.

It was a leftover from the start, or rather a potpourri of practically every style known to Los Angeles. The tower soars like an Egyptian obelisk, but then there's something Hellenistic-Byzantine about it, too. It is encrusted with relief statuary of literary greats and is inscribed here, there, and everywhere with library-esque sayings (as well as more current graffiti). The proponents of modern cityscape architecture are constantly seeking ways to destroy Goodhue's charming little library. They've already turned its formal gardens into parking space. But the library is a marvelous conglomerate structure, an enduring and integral part of downtown Los Angeles.

## The Biltmore Hotel (right)
### 515 South Olive Street

I love cities, and I love city streets, but Pershing Square, which faces the Biltmore, is not a nice place to be. And I hate to say that—I don't want to frighten people away from the city. But as I drew I watched a knife-wielding madman slashing a date palm and screaming at the air. Eventually the cops pulled up, searching for the creature, who in the meantime had screamed on down a side street. And there were *cholos* being frisked by the police, who had lined them up in front of a grimy fountain. The *cholos*, too, had menacing knives in their baggy pockets.

The poor Biltmore faces all this craziness. (To be fair, on another drawing day, a warm and comfortable Sunday, Pershing Square was not unpleasant.) The setting was nicer, I'm sure, in 1923, when the Schultze and Weaver design was opened to the public. The interior is famous for its elegance, rehabilitated now in all its barrel-vaulted, Spanish Renaissance glory and hand-painted detail. Like much of twenties L.A., the hotel is very Beaux Arts (a term for the early-twentieth-century style that uses classical decorative art forms on the curtain walls of a modern structure).

It's an L.A. castle like the Bonaventure—but the Biltmore, sadly, has no concrete bastions for protection.

The Biltmore on Olive Street Downtown Los Angeles July 3, 1983 Robert Miles Parker

**The *Times* Building** (*right*)
**Corner of Spring and First Streets**

The *Los Angeles Times* is one of America's great newspapers—a monumental institution housed in a monumental Deco structure. The building, designed by Gordon B. Kaufmann (1931-35), has the look of a temple, or maybe of great praying hands. It suggests that herein reside truth and freedom of expression: the nobility of the printed word.

In the early seventies, Los Angeles architect William Pereira added his touch to the *Times*. It's quite readable. A successful blending of styles always pleases me, and Pereira has arranged a good match between his modern flying wing and the solid, solemn older building. The horizontality of Kaufmann's Attic temple is repeated by Pereira's addition. The *moderne* effects of soaring engaged columns, rows of vertical windows, and the decorative chevrons are all complemented by the new wing's horizontal windows and railings. Pereira's addition is folded into the old *Times* building, further enhancing the original Deco stair-step design. It's a successful amalgam of the work of two masters.

**The Oviatt Building** (*left*)
**617 South Olive Street**

The Oviatt Building epitomizes the glory of twenties-renaissance L.A. The building was designed as a Romanesque castle (1927-28) by Walker and Eisen. It is studded with balcony cresting, balustrades, and a campanile-like tower. The first floor and the marquee are a tribute to the magic of Lalique: the building houses a spectacular collection of Lalique glass—perhaps the best glass collection in the city.

Mr. Oviatt luxuriated in the penthouse atop this princely downtown structure, from which he could survey all the other castles popping up on the landscape.

THE
TIMES
BUILDING
ROBERT
MILES PARKER
JULY 29, 1983
1ST STREET
L.A.

**The Coca-Cola Bottling Company**
**1334 South Central**

The Coca-Cola Bottling Company must be one of the five most peculiar buildings in L.A. The structure existed for a long time before it became a steamship. That didn't occur until the late thirties when Robert Derrah "streamlined" the old factories. It has been suggested that the then president of the company, Mr. Barbe, was a nautical enthusiast. The streamline *moderne* style reflected his love of the sea, as well as his insistence that Coca-Cola's bottling methods be clean and spiffy.

What a kick to be driving up the boulevard and suddenly find this sleek oceanliner gliding toward you. It is still a resplendent vessel with its bridge, metal railing, ship's doors, porthole windows, and metal rivets.

**St. Vincent Court**
**Off Seventh Street, between Broadway
and Hill**

An Armenian workman, while taking
a break, proudly told me the story of St.
Vincent Court. "It seems," he said, "that
there were once gates at what is now the
entry to the Court. They marked the edge
of Los Angeles city, and there was a little
church, St. Vincent's. In 1906, Bullock's was
constructed—you're looking at the back of
it. It and the other surrounding stores turned
St. Vincent Court into an alley."

Carved into an alcove of Bullock's is the
Pasquini Espresso Shop. It's been there twenty-
five years. Mr. Pasquini explains, "Bullock's
was gonna have a summer sale and they
asked me to sell espresso. I been here ever
since." His espresso is the best in town—
everyone knows that. In fact, Mr. Pasquini's
wares are famous as far away as South
America and Europe. Just ask him, he'll
tell you. His alcove is a haven for Italian-
Americans. In the late afternoon they cluster
around little tables to stake out a bit of Rome.
They play cards, puff cigarettes, and drink
espresso.

This part of downtown is changing
rapidly. Bullock's will soon become part of a
new jewelry mart. Mr. Pasquini doesn't know
what will happen to his espresso stand. "Here
today, tomorrow who knows?" he shrugs.

**The Maplewood
902 Maple Street**

**1126 Mignonette Street** (*above*)

Driving into the city just the other day, I did a double take. This old house was gone! In fact, the whole street was gone. Fast-paced L.A. had sent the residents off to different ramshackle houses on another side of town, I suppose.

**Incomplete Building with Onion Domes** (*left*)

In all directions, though sometimes only in a passing glimpse from the freeway, you can spot the splendors of L.A. architecture. Forget the traffic snarls and forget the cars creeping too slowly—just look to the side. You might see a Buddhist temple, or perhaps Mt. Vernon. Or maybe Middle Eastern onion domes on a downtown apartment house.

**Victorian with Porch Towers** (*left*)
**633 West Fifteenth Street**

The first "American" style of architecture to flourish in Los Angeles was the Victorian Queen Anne. The citizens who arrived in the boom of the 1880s didn't think much of the architectural heritage they found. Mexican was not fine enough. It was much more fashionable to create architecture in the mode of the old homeland—for these folks that meant the American Midwest.

Absurdly glorious Victorian houses circled the original Los Angeles pueblo and the newer downtown. The most unfortunate example of the demise of the Victorians is, of course, Bunker Hill. It's been stripped of its Victorian "mess" and is now sleek and modern. But much of Victorian L.A. still lurks about. Perhaps the most spectacular example is Carroll Avenue in Angelino Heights. But there are all sorts of buildings hiding around central Los Angeles, left behind on side streets that few people know about. The most interesting attempt to preserve them is Heritage Square, the new site to which some of these Victorian dowagers have been moved.

These structures reflect the days of conspicuous consumption. The buildings were designed to show everyone the latest whimsies and most imaginative appendages the owner could afford. The more complex the building, the happier the builder. Fortunately, Victorians have come back into vogue, and many of the remaining pieces are being lovingly restored.

**Old Victorian** (*right*)
**629 West Eighteenth Street**

ROBERT MILES PARKER · JULY 22, 1983

THE SHRINE AUDITORIUM ON ROYAL STREET, OF COURSE

**The First AME Church** (left)
**6200 South Harvard**
**University Heights**

Though its current structure does not hint at
the fact, the First AME Methodist Church is the
oldest black congregation in Los Angeles. It is
also probably the largest black church in
L.A., boasting over 3,000 members. The
current structure was completed by Paul R.
Williams, a well-known Los Angeles black
architect.

**The Coliseum** (below)
**Exposition Park**

The Mussolini-*moderne* Los Angeles Memorial Coliseum was designed
by John and Donald B. Parkinson (1921-23). It's oval and big. The home
of the 1932 Olympics, the structure is being spruced up again to be an
Olympic host in 1984.

**The Shrine Auditorium** (left)
**Jefferson Boulevard and Royal Street**

You know how the Shriners love to have fun. It's no wonder they built
a temple that's reminiscent of an Islamic circus. In the early twenties,
they commissioned John C. Austin, A.M. Edelman, and G.A.
Lansburgh to build their auditorium. The edifice resembles a puffed-
up balloon of pita bread with Arabic icing dripping out the edges.
The towers, with their decorative moons and stars, are like candles on
the Shriners' temple cake.

   This mad conglomeration is officially called the Al Malai Kah
Temple, long one of L.A.'s major auditoriums.

**The Osiris Apartments** (*below*)
**430 Union Avenue**

I think the buildings wedged between downtown and Hollywood are the most exciting in the city. If you love cities, love the urban landscape, love architecture, then it's really better to drive the freeways, because if you use the surface streets in this area, you'll be so distracted you'll never reach your destination.

Here's an apartment building named for the Egyptian god of life. Twenties revival architecture constantly surprises us. Each building is a fantasy on a theme. This part of town teems with all kinds of people, all kinds of architectural styles. Teems with life. Hail, Osiris!

**The Doria Apartments** (*above*)
**1600–1608 West Pico Boulevard**
**Alvarado Terrace, Westlake**

There's no way you can drive past without this building grabbing your attention. Big and smooth, it looms over the street life. It watches, bemused. And the street life is fun—very Mexican and so very appropriate to this mission revival style of apartment building. That style was a romantic look at California's Spanish-Mexican heritage. It's good that the Doria is now a hub for that same community.

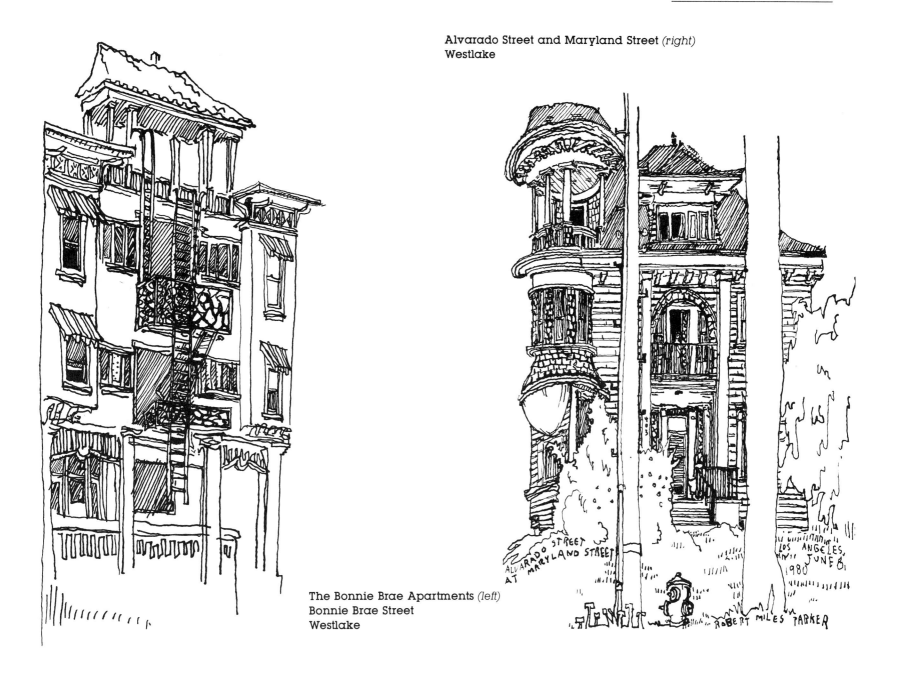

**Alvarado Street and Maryland Street** *(right)*
Westlake

**The Bonnie Brae Apartments** *(left)*
Bonnie Brae Street
Westlake

**The American Storage Company** (*below*)
**Junction of Beverly Boulevard, Council Street, and Temple Street**
**MacArthur Park—North**

The American Storage Company, a Spanish Colonial revival tower, has fascinated Angelenos since its construction in 1929. (The architect was Arthur E. Harvey.) It seems to be preparing for takeoff, the envy of all those Angelenos sitting on the Hollywood Freeway and wistfully watching.

**The Bonnie Brae House** (*above*)
**818 South Bonnie Brae Street**
**Westlake**

With its Moorish tower topped off by absurd spindles, its windows framed in quizzical eyebrows, and its billowy fish-scale skirts, the Bonnie Brae House is the most glorious Victorian edifice in Los Angeles. It is the supreme example of the 1880s principle: ostentatious opulence is best.

**The Mailing House**
**356 South Western Avenue**

These L.A. buildings with giant unnecessary towers are not just poorly camouflaged innuendoes. They are that, and here the architecture seems an apt pun on the name of the company and its wares. But that's not the whole story. Towers like this one were created to attract the motorist. Detroit may not believe it, but L.A. is Motor City. Motorists driving past could see those towers thrust up into the (then) blue sky. Like magnets, the towers pulled the cars in. Wily merchandizing, L.A. style.

**The Normandy Apartment House** *(right)*
**130 Westmoreland Avenue**
**Westlake**

"We like this building like it was my mother." Well, anybody would. It's easy to imagine the building when it was fashionable. It's a marvelous Norman castle set in a nowhere land. But now nowhere has become the land of the *cholos.*

There are the 18th Street Gang, the Diamond Gang, the Rosebushes, and the AC/DC's. You see their symbols on lots of walls. These are the local *cholos,* the gangs. And then there are the Chokers—"they live up in the trees, with a clubhouse," and are remembered for breaking all of the roof glass in the apartment building. Little Earl, in the upstairs window, is the chronicler for both his beloved castle and the knights of *cholo*-land. For him the gangs are street lore, part of the history of the neighborhood—part of the history of L.A.

**California Federal Savings** *(left)*
**270 North Vermont**
**MacArthur Park—North**

There are mock Mt. Vernons everywhere in Los Angeles. This Mt. Vernon (Rick Farver Associates, 1960), however, is an exact replica of Washington's house (although I don't think George and Martha had a "Drive-up Window" sign.) The lantern is even four inches off center, just like the original.

It's noteworthy that this reproduction of the home of the Father of Our Country is in a sleazy area of town. It sits on disputed turf; feuding gangs scrawl their advertisements on its walls. The graffiti pile up so quickly that the exterior needs repainting every three months.

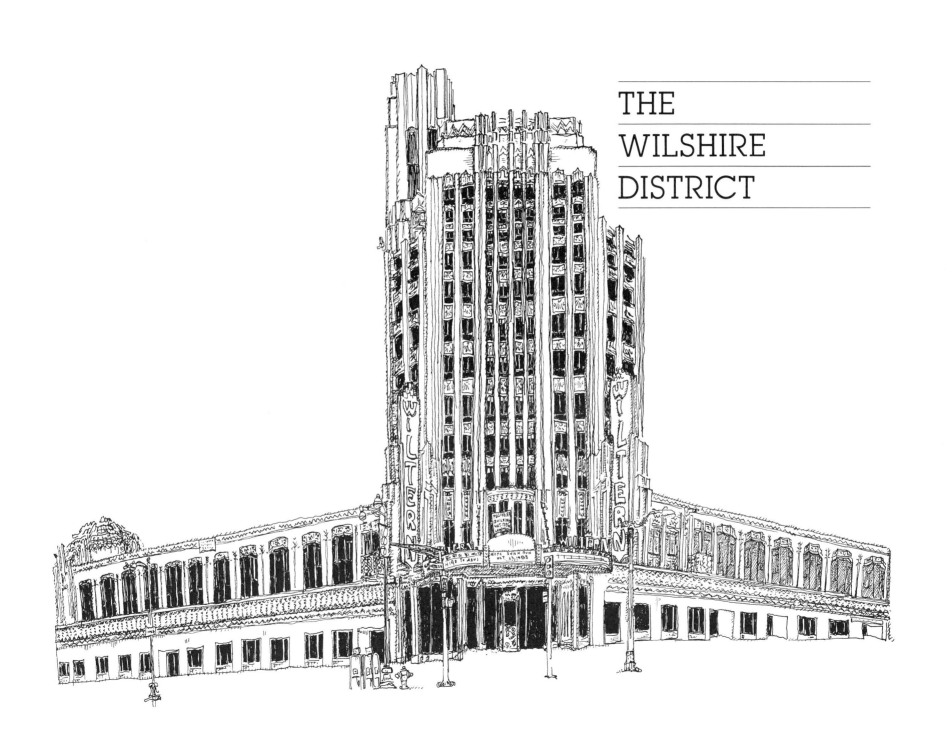

THE
WILSHIRE
DISTRICT

**The El Rey Theater**
**5515 Wilshire Boulevard**

The El Rey is the relic of a time when cinema was quite stylish. In this case, the style used (by architect W. Clifford Balch) was high *moderne*. The huge "El Rey" in the sky and the zigzag lines accenting the front panels carry your eye down to the marquee. The decorative insets on the face of the building—with their crazy patterns of flowers, lightning bolts, and hunks of fruit—are similar to the carpets spread across the lobbies of all the great old theaters. They're little pictures hinting at the multifarious splendors of the big picture inside.

The El Rey is still a popular movie house, even though it now features second runs. And everyone still loves the building as the symbol of a magic time long past.

**The Pellissier Building and Wiltern Theater**
*(overleaf)*
**Wilshire and Western**

Among aficionados, the 1931 Pellissier Building by Morgan, Walls, and Clements is, without a doubt, the most popular of the Los Angeles Deco masterpieces. It is a twelve-story dandy, resplendent in turquoise terra-cotta. The tower is one of the most famous of those many Deco exclamation points punctuating the Los Angeles sky.

### The Bella Vista Apartments and Shops
### 1617 Wilshire Boulevard

The Bella Vista sits on a part of Wilshire Boulevard awash in bag people and leftover beauties. The second story is a beauty itself, from the days of the neoclassic/Southern revival style. The Boulevard went commercial in the forties, whence the Bella Vista shop fronts.

The shops and apartments together form a little neighborhood.

Once Mexican, the locals are now mostly Salvadoran. At the Cuscatlan Cafe, you can get a genuine *chorizo salvadoreño*, and to go with it they recommend a big tall plastic container of "rice drink." Both very tasty.

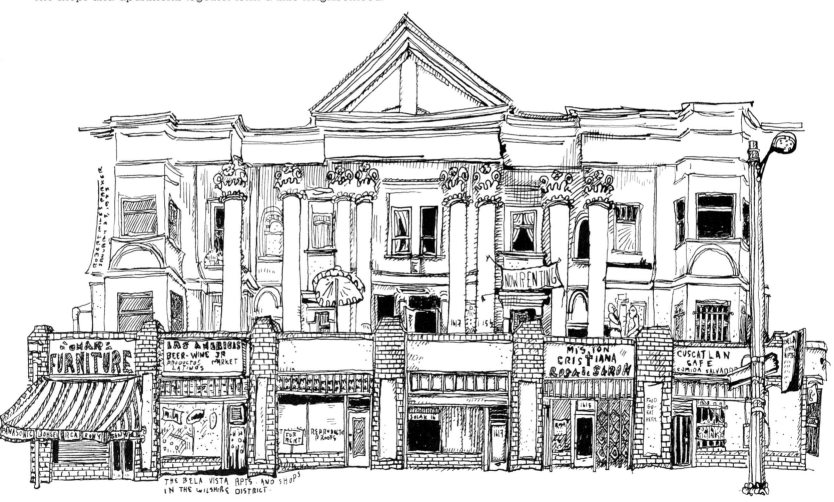

## Bullock's Wilshire
## Wilshire and Westmoreland

If you only do one other adventuresome thing in your life, go to the Bullock's on Wilshire. It is the most glorious department store in Los Angeles, perhaps in the West, maybe even in the United States.

The structure's design elements were based on the Art Deco concept imported from the *Ars Décoratifs* Paris exhibit of 1925. Each part of the structure is also a piece of art. Bullock's also follows the Deco concept of incorporating the automobile as an integral part of the composition. It was constructed in 1929 (architects, John and Donald B. Parkinson), when Wilshire Boulevard was still a rather new place, a motorized suburb. John D. Bullock designed his store to attract wealthy, chauffered clientele from Hancock Park and other smart areas.

The main entrance to all this Deco dazzle is from the rear, under a porte cochere that has a ceiling mural by Herman Sachs entitled "The Spirit of Transportation." The mural acts as a prelude to the symphony of art that fills Bullock's. The interior is lavishly grand. Walls in the elevator lobby are rose marble, highlighted by bronze, copper, and gunmetal.

As you have every right to expect in surroundings like these, the service is impeccable.

**The Old Tom Bergin's** (*below*)
**6100 Block of Wilshire**

This building, a fine example of Tudor revival, makes expert use of brick patterns and half-timber crisscrosses. The windows are fun, all shapes and sizes, the kind you like to look out of.

Bergin's Bar was once the star attraction here. It's now around the corner in a building not half so nice. The current tenants range from artists and advertising people in the lofts to an artificial fingernail specialist and an astrologist down below.

**The Brown Derby** (*above*)
**Corner of Wilshire and Alexandria**

The Brown Derby was built in 1926, a time when Los Angeles was happy to be going wonderfully mad. The Derby was the place to see and be seen. That time has gone, and the Derby is too—almost. It now sits in vacant disrepair, anxiously peeping from under its brim for the approaching wrecking ball.

**A Shaggy House** (*below*)
**314 Manhattan Place**

This is a marvelous example of Craftsman architecture. The lines borrowed from Greene and Greene prototypes in Pasadena still suggest a marriage of Western open space, Swiss rooflines, and a touch of Japan. The mid-Wilshire District is full of buildings like this, many of them now in sad repair. What was once a comfortable and smart neighborhood has become a dumping ground for new people in town. The original owners are probably now living in a Valley replica of one of these glorious Craftsman buildings.

**St. Andrews Place**
**333 South St. Andrews Place**

This is what has replaced all those wonderful Greene and Greene style homes.

**The Mutual of Omaha Building**
**5225 Wilshire Boulevard**

The Mutual of Omaha Building was originally called the E. Clem Wilson Building. It was designed in 1930 by Meyer and Holler. The structure sits at a grand intersection on Wilshire Boulevard, a proud monument to Deco styling. Angelenos should be proud of it, too. It's better looking than the Mutual of Omaha building in Omaha.

## Park La Brea
### Between Third and Sixth at Curson

Park La Brea is a well trimmed, very Jewish piece of New York, picked up and plopped down in the middle of L.A. There are eighteen towers and twenty-four blocks of "garden apartments." What I've always loved about Park La Brea is the way the sun and the shadows hit those stark walls. The towers remind me of smokestacks standing in an empty field—a modern Stonehenge.

The project was begun shortly before World War II, or so the blue-haired ladies in the elevator told me, and both the garden apartments and the steel frames for the towers had been constructed when the war commenced. After the war, the towers were completed.

Approximately 16,000 people live on the 176 acres. The residents are invariably polite, some have European accents, many are professionals respected in their fields. It's a complete community and seems as safe as a medieval fortress.

## Dog and Cat Hospital
## 940 North Highland Avenue

Only in Los Angeles would they perch a neon dalmatian on a stucco pediment. And only in Los Angeles would there be a bas relief of bird dogs in cattail marshes eyeballing ducks overhead. It all makes wonderful sense—it's a dog and cat hospital. Pets were very big in Deco L.A.

The theme continues inside with more relief work—Scotties scurrying up stairwells, snakes peering around banisters, and elephants stomping through hallways. Lassie is there, of course. And the typical Deco lady, a hissing cat arched against her leg, a barking dog nearby.

No bland building this. Nowadays, you can't tell a dog and cat hospital from a dentist's office.

**Meaty Meat Burgers**
**Corner of Pico and Fairfax**

I was driving along in a dreadful mood. It was afternoon rush hour, drizzly, gray, and I hated L.A. And suddenly— the Meaty Meat Burgers sign jumped out at me! A stubby tree points to a row of ziggurats, and the City of Hope's ziggurat points to that audacious billboard. Los Angeles is nothing if not blatant. And so I fell in love with it again.

The Meaty Meat Burgers stand, its neighboring shops, and even the silly billboard are the quintessential statement of L.A. pedestrian architecture. And there's something very human about them—funny, vulgar, and alive.

## Fairfax
## 400 Block, North Fairfax Avenue

They came as if still in search of the Promised Land—the march of
Jewish immigrants through the city is legend, as are their
contributions, both cultural and commercial. One still finds a hint of
Jewish culture in old Boyle Heights. Certainly Park La Brea is "Little
Manhattan." And the Valley, as everyone knows, is Very Jewish. But
in Los Angeles proper, the street is Fairfax. That's where the best
Jewish food can be had, and that's where you can still see
yarmulkes and peyes even on a weekday.

## The Pan Pacific Building
## Curson Avenue

How disheartening to watch one of the world's great streamline-*moderne* pieces of architecture crumble. For years the Pan Pacific was home for many Hollywood fetes and extravaganzas. And now it merely languishes on a forgotten back street.

The auditorium was built in 1935 by Wurdeman and Becket; from the very beginning it was a quintessential symbol of Los Angeles. Its four flagpole pylons repeat a nautical theme that is omnipresent in the great dry valley of Los Angeles, a city yearning for contact with the sea. Though it lacked a natural harbor, L.A. always wanted to be taken seriously as a port. At least it could proclaim its nautical aspiration in its architecture.

The Pan Pacific is eroding now beneath the tides of time.

5675 FIRESTONE BOULEVARD
THE CITY OF COMMERCE

ROBERT MILES PARKER · JUNE 19, 1983

**The Samson Tyre and Rubber Company** *(overleaf)*
**5675 Telegraph Road**
**Commerce**

The whole city of Commerce could use this place for its offices, fire station, health center, orphanage, and grocery store. It has got to be the most vast and marvelous building in all of the Los Angeles area. And it's empty.

The structure was slated for destruction, a new hotel to rise from its ashes. However, those hordes of Orange County commuters heard of the impending doom of the Samson Tyre and Rubber Company building and raised a cry louder than the roar of the freeways. They wanted their monument to stay. The city of Commerce listened to the commuters—now the old place will be transformed into a hotel, its facade left intact.

This Assyrian temple was originally the second largest tire manufacturing plant in the world. It was designed by Morgan, Walls, and Clements and built in 1929. Adolf Schleicher himself, it is assumed, chose this motif to immortalize his company's name: The Samson Tyre and Rubber Company. It's appropriate that a tire manufacturing palace ended up facing the Santa Ana Freeway, one of the world's busiest.

The ziggurat-like palace, with its rows of rolling wheels and its bas-relief gods, has delighted me since I was a little boy. Everyone should sit in front of this castle, back to the freeway, and listen to the roar. And listen, also, to the silence of this old dream.

**L.A. Oil Fields**
**View of the 4700 Block**
**of South La Cienega**
**Baldwin Hills**

Baldwin Hills is almost the geographic center of Los Angeles. How fitting, then, that here should sit a field of oil wells, pumping some of that lifeblood that enables the city to live.

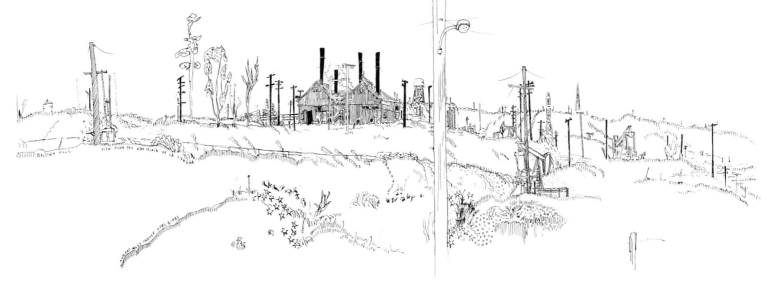

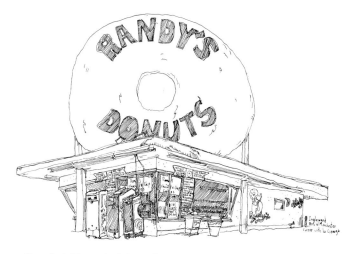

**Randy's Donuts** (*above*)
**805 West Manchester**
**Inglewood**

Inglewood is a town built during the boom of 1887. As was usual in those days, first a large hotel was built—then a bust followed soon after. There's something special about Inglewood, though: Randy's Donuts, born in 1954.

There were once three such donuts decorating Los Angeles. Randy's, a survivor, sits as a lonely sentinel above the San Diego Freeway.

**The Gill Railway Station** (*below*)
**Cabrillo Avenue and Torrance Boulevard**
**Torrance**

Irving Gill designed the Torrance Pacific Electric Railway Station in 1913. Actually, there are Gill structures all over Torrance. You can get a glimpse of his elegant railroad bridge on one side of the station. Gill's work is important because he simplified the California style to *moderne*—flat walls pierced with shadowed recesses and supported by functional, nondecorative columns.

On the other side of the station, you now get a glimpse of a car wash, and the railway station itself is boarded up and deserted.

**The Carson Teen Post** (below)
**21832 Main Street**
**Carson**

Carson must be a dreary place, but I can't say for sure—I never could find it. Main Street, which runs from downtown L.A. almost to the ocean, is a monotonous prospect in the stretch between the "Welcome to Carson" and "You're now leaving Carson" signs. About the only interesting building for twenty minutes in each direction is the Carson Teen Post. And it's a mess.

**The Lynwood Pacific Electric Station** (left)
**Fernwood Avenue and Long Beach Boulevard**
**Lynwood**

Freeways were not the first means of mass transportation in metropolitan Los Angeles. That distinction belongs to the Pacific Electric Railway System. The Lynwood Station (early 1900s) was a stop on the way from Santa Ana to downtown Los Angeles.

There's a melancholy feeling about Lynwood these days. It doesn't feel much like a town now—more like one huge waiting room, as if everyone were waiting for the old Pacific Electric to come through and take them away.

Like the town's present-day population, Lynwood Station is an architectural "Duke's Mix." It has hints of California Craftsman, a neoclassic portico, and even touches of both late Victorian and mission revival.

**The Watts Towers** (right)
**1765 107th Street**
**Watts**

The Towers of Simon Rodia are no doubt the most absurdly wonderful pieces of architecture in Los Angeles. Constructed from 1921 to 1954, the Towers are internationally acclaimed as folk fantasy masterpieces.

Over the course of many years, Simon Rodia, an Italian immigrant, built these mad things—simply because he had to, as a gesture of gratitude to his adopted nation. Then, one day, he up and left. Years later, he was discovered in northern California and, when asked about his mysterious departure, replied, "What else do you do when your wife dies?" That answer is as puzzling as his work. The construct is a series of towers that soar hundreds of feet into the sky. They're built of steel-reinforced concrete and decorated with Los Angeles leftovers: broken tile, china, Seven-Up bottles. Somehow, it all works together to create a great vision.

The city, thinking they were a public danger, once tried to pull them down but failed—the towers were too well built. So they were made into an official monument. Unofficially they are a monument too—to the nation, the imagination, and man's peculiar need to build.

**Moorish Apartments**
**6921 Middleton Street**
**Huntington Park**

Huntington Park is the first "real city" south of downtown—it has a main street full of busy shoppers and side streets lined with typical, nondescript apartment dwellings.

This particular apartment building, however, is not so typical. A free-form Islamic delight, it harkens back to the more playful twenties and thirties, when architects amused themselves and us by borrowing styles from all over the world.

**Temple Bethel** (*above*)
**3000 Southern Avenue**
**South Gate**

South Gate and Lynwood, Compton and Huntington Park—they're a line of cities that were once comfortable, middle-class communities. They still boast some very good vernacular architecture, particularly Deco and *moderne*. The cities now range from multi-racial, working-class places bereft of civic pride to multi-racial, working-class towns that reflect a concern for the community.

South Gate is about as blue-collar a town as you can find in Los Angeles. Right smack in the middle of it is this charming "lighthouse for God," Temple Bethel.

**Casa de Governor Pio Pico**
**Pioneer Boulevard**
**Whittier**

It wasn't all that long ago that the governors of California lived in homes like this one. Pio Pico's casa was constructed in 1850 and rebuilt in 1883-84. It's an understated Mexican adobe with covered walkways. The neighborhood is not a nice one now. Next door is a vacant lot littered with gravestones. Behind the house is a one-time river—now a mud pie with trash cans swimming in it. Of course there's a freeway, and some railroad tracks too. A sad collection of neighbors for the home of the last Mexican governor.

**The Tamale**
**6421 Whittier Boulevard**
**Montebello**

There was a time in American architectural history when people built for chuckles. That time is not now. The Casa Garcia not only makes the passerby smile—it also makes him want to munch a tamale. Right there in the heart of Montebello's industrial landscape.

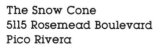

**The Snow Cone**
**5115 Rosemead Boulevard**
**Pico Rivera**

This was once a popcorn and peanut stand. Then it was a battery stand. (Can you believe that?) Now it's a Cosmic Ice stand. Vivian and Lewis Moye have owned the place for two years now. Soon, I suppose, there will be robots selling computers here.

BETWEEN THE RIVER AND GREGG ROAD · PICO RIVERA · JUNE 26, 1983 ·ROBERT MILES PARKER

**Mt. Baldy Inn**
**Whittier Boulevard**
**Pico Rivera**

There's the real Mt. Baldy, and then there's the one right across
the river from Pio Pico's old house. It hunches in sad disarray on
Whittier Boulevard, watching greased lowriders patrol the street. The
mountain was constructed in lath and plaster (how L.A.—"a
mountain was constructed"!) in 1927 as the Mt. Baldy Inn. It has seen
use not only as an inn but also as a disco palace and a pizza parlor.
Now it's deserted.

**The Neff Caretaker's House**
**Neff Park**
**La Mirada**

La Mirada, like most towns surrounding L.A.,
was once farms and groves of olives, lemons,
and oranges. This old house was the
caretaker's place for a farm of over 2OO
acres. A restful sight for eyes weary of smog-
shrouded Los Angeles.

**County General Hospital** (*overleaf*)
**State Street**
**Lincoln Heights**

The County Hospital looks like a hospital should—a great Romanesque cathedral, a place of rest and renewal for the sick and weary. You feel uplifted just approaching the grand porticoed doorways. Relief statues of medical greats and other heroes (including an angel of mercy) watch over the entrance.

The medical center was designed between 1928 and 1933 by the Allied Architects of Los Angeles. The twenty-story central unit is a major city landmark.

CORNER OF CHICAGO STREET AND MICHIGAN AVENUE IN BOYLE HEIGHTS, LOS ANGELES - AUGUST 7, 1979 - ROBERT MILES PARKER

**The Church of Christian Hope**
**Chicago Street and Michigan Avenue**
**Boyle Heights**

Once a predominantly Jewish suburb, Boyle Heights is now predominantly a wild and visually stimulating potpourri. Its history and its present conglomerate population of Chicanos, Blacks, and Asians all contribute to the effect.

The Church of Christian Hope, constructed in 1905, symbolizes the wild and woolly wonder of Boyle Heights then and now. Bordered in barbed wire, it is a crazy quilt of architectural styles, ranging from Islamic to pueblo. Cap it off with that marvelous billboard—Angelenos love to advertise.

**The Cummings Block** (below)
**Corner of Boyle and First Streets**
**Boyle Heights**

Boyle Heights was once a Jewish neighborhood—Max Factor grew up there. And there are still hints of that old time.

Fay Sheller, who resides in the area, rambles: "...so where else to go? We have our gravestone almost ready. Everyone is here... well, one brother is at Mt. Sinai, but I don't know anyone else out there. I don't know anywhere else to live. I came here as a young girl... my brothers, my sisters.... Somewhere else I'd be the old lady next door, but here I'm somebody. This is a good place."

**Lincoln Hospital** (above)
**443 Soto Street**
**Boyle Heights**

Lincoln Hospital is one of the oldest hospitals in Los Angeles, having served Boyle Heights since 1904. Its antecedent is the German Hospital Society, which was founded with a $20,000 endowment by Louise Werner in 1903. The original German name can still be seen on the cornerstone, and the design of the little Victorian edifice is lifted directly from the illustration of a hospital in Germany, pictured on the hospital's charter.

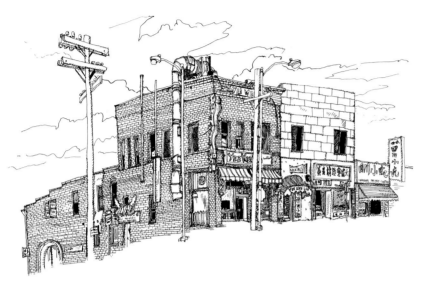

**Chinatown View**
**Corner of Spring and Ord Streets**
**Chinatown**

L.A.'s Chinatown began after the gold rush and expanded as new immigrants arrived with the railroad boom in the 1880s. The area experienced growth yet a third time from the 1890s on through the teens. Originally, Chinatown had its center where Union Station now stands. When the station was built, the Chinese were pushed slightly northwards.

Much of today's Chinatown is a gaudy, pagodaed tourist package. This particular view is, perhaps, more honest. And the Yee Mee Loo restaurant is famous for the autographed photos of thirties and forties movie stars on its walls.

**Old Warehouses**
**Main and College**
**Olvera Street Area**

**Pico House** (*right*)
**Main Street**

In 1870, Pio Pico, the last Mexican governor of California, commissioned Ezra Kysor to create this very "uptown" hotel. It was the city's first three-story structure and is an excellent example of commercial Italianate architecture.

The Pico House represents the first in the line of Victorian styles that, for a while at least, converted Los Angeles into an Eastern city, one that denied its Mexican heritage. It's an interesting sidelight that the last Mexican governor of California built the first large-scale Anglo-American building.

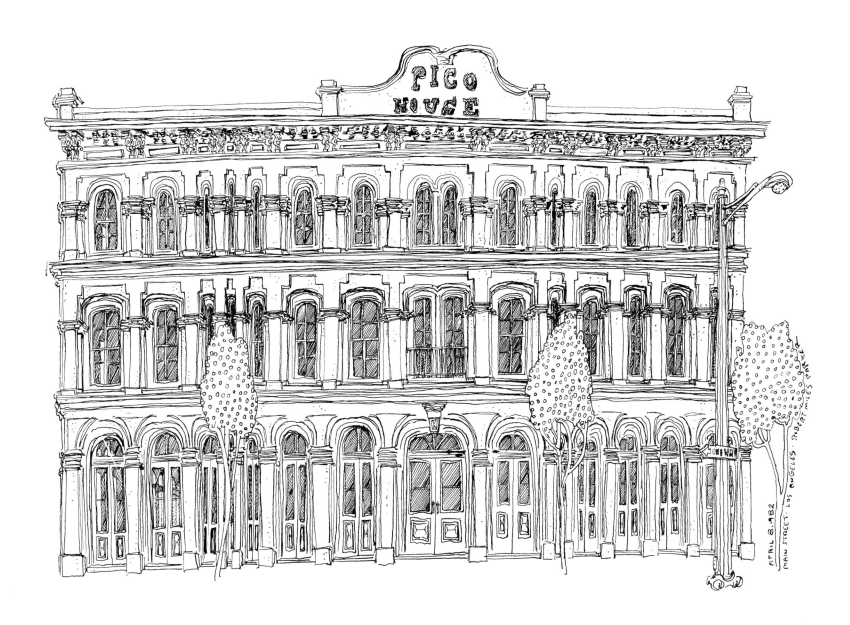

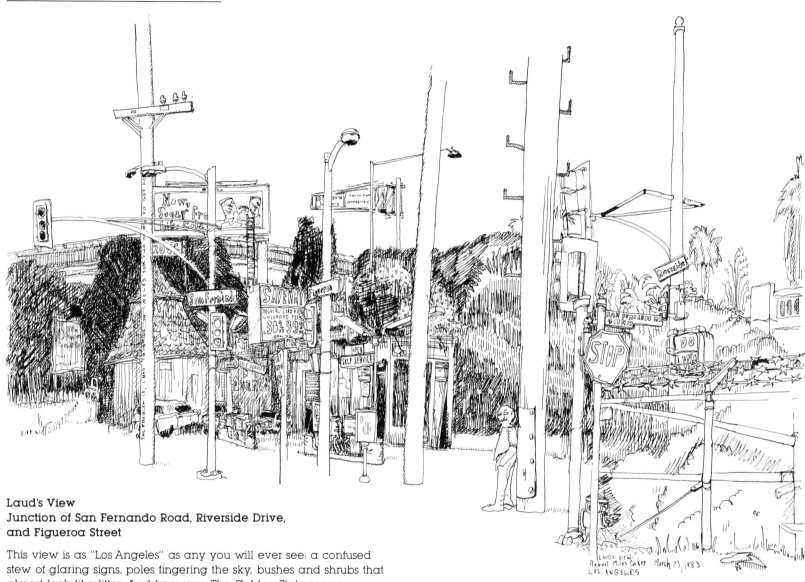

**Laud's View
Junction of San Fernando Road, Riverside Drive,
and Figueroa Street**

This view is as "Los Angeles" as any you will ever see: a confused
stew of glaring signs, poles fingering the sky, bushes and shrubs that
almost look like litter. And freeways. The Golden State zooms
overhead; the Pasadena flies off to one side; just off view the
Glendale springs from one freeway and the Harbor from the other.
The Hollywood's down there too, somewhere. L.A. jumble.

**The Goldberg House** (left)
**3739 Mayfair Drive**
**Mt. Washington**

Mt. Washington and its neighbor, Highland Park, were originally part of the Rancho San Rafael. Development began in the 1880s. Highland Park was the second area to be annexed to the original Los Angeles city boundaries, in an effort to establish law and order. There were notorious roadhouses all through the arroyo. Highland Park started life as a den of thieves.

The two areas are loaded with great, semi-great, and pedestrian architecture. With ease, you can find mission revival castles, Victorian cottages, and modern "machines for living." 3739 Mayfair Drive, resting on top of Mt. Washington, is an excellent example of the modern style. It affords a comfortable view extending from downtown out to the valleys, and its exterior blends well with the natural and imported vegetation.

**The Van de Kamp's Bakery Building** (right)
**2930 Fletcher Drive**
**Glassell Park**

The Van de Kamp's Bakery Building looks like it should. A good reflection of proper, clean, Dutch attitudes. And it seems all the more prim and proper here in a rather disreputable section of town. Van de Kamp's began as a family enterprise, and there's still a family feel about it. Employees enthusiastically puff their goods while they bake the goodies. The business began in 1915 with the manufacturing and selling of "Saratoga Chips." Now over two hundred items come from Van de Kamp's ovens.

The bakery, modeled on a typical Dutch townhouse design, was built in 1931. It's an island of pleasant aromas and kitchen coziness in a neighborhood of asphalt and roaring streets.

**The B & J Sewing Machine Company Building** *(below)*
**Figueroa Street and Cypress Avenue**
**Highland Park**

The B & J Sewing Machine Company is the sort of building that tells the story of a community. At the turn of the century, Figueroa must have been a pleasant residential street. Note the dormers peeking from above the commercial facade. They suggest a cozy Craftsman cottage, a family home. Look at the building now, with its boxlike front. The tiling seems to have been added in the thirties, when the sewing machine company was born. The street and the B & J Building are getting shoddy now, getting lost in the Angeleno rush to someplace else.

**The Sparkletts Water Building** *(below)*
**4500 Lincoln**
**Eagle Rock**

I don't exactly know what to say about Eagle Rock. It's just another suburb wedged between the city and Pasadena. Some buildings are eye-pleasers, some are eyesores. The most delightful of its surprises is the Sparkletts Building.

The structure was designed and constructed between 1925 and 1929 by Mr. King. It aptly embodies the twenties preoccupation with exotic "other cultures."

The Sparkletts water is right inside; the springs bubble up beneath those Arabian domes. Oriental romance in Eagle Rock.

**The Bucket** (*left*)
4541 Eagle Rock Boulevard
Eagle Rock

Here's an excellent example of thirties whimsy. It was designed to look like a lunch bucket; you can still see the gizmo the handle hooked to.

The restaurant seats ten people—a real crowd when everybody is getting his hamburger. The burgers are piled with cheese, avocado, tomatoes ("What, you don't like tomatoes? You eat 'em—they're good for you!"), lettuce, onions, and dripping sauce.

Julio Maeso runs The Bucket. He's been there eight years and is famous for his grumpy demeanor. He presides over a greasy counter, almost as greasy as the food he serves. Now, don't get me wrong—this food is wonderful. On a wilted, soggy paper plate he piles french fries glopped with an audacious sauce. Julio demands that you have a beer, too. I suggest you recover with a nap. That's exactly what I did.

The *National Enquirer* says, "The Bucket serves the world's rudest hamburger." Julio does seem to pride himself on being a grouch. But between you and me, he's not. He may be famous for flashing a butcher knife and yelling a lot, but he insisted that as a poor, struggling artist I take my extra potatoes home in a brown bag. "These potatoes healthy, good for you!"

**Sunset and Beaudry** (*below*)
Elysian Park
(The Stephen McCarroll Memorial Drawing)

Los Angeles never stands still—the city is always flexing and wiggling. This row of apartments has already been muscled out of existence.

SUNSET AND BEAUDRY · MAY 15, 1982 · ROBERT MILES PARKER

View across Sunset Boulevard
Angeleno Heights

**View from Echo Park Avenue**
**Echo Park**

**Angelus Temple**
**Park and Glendale**
**Echo Park**

Aimee Semple McPherson's temple was built from her own designs in 1923. She arrived in Los Angeles in 1918, and from then until her death she was one of the city's stellar characters. She might be called the Terry Cole Whittaker of her time (or vice versa). She had thousands of followers and no trouble making lots of money. Her temple, designed like a Broadway theater with rows of tiered seats dropping to the orchestra pit, holds 5,300 people. When McPherson died in 1944, she left the ministry in the care of her son, Rolf, who, in 1972, refurbished the Angelus Temple.

**The Ennis-Brown House**
**2607 Glendower Avenue**
**Los Feliz**

The most glorious Frank Lloyd Wright house
in all of Los Angeles is the Ennis-Brown. It is
without doubt the most monumental of all
Wright's concrete-block houses. Constructed
in 1924, this reborn Mayan temple commands
a spectacular hillside view. Of the two recur-
rent themes in Los Angeles, the nautical and
the Mayan, the Ennis-Brown House sings that
second strange tune. It's hard to understand
why Los Angeles loves Mayan architecture—
the jungle is even further from L.A. than the
ocean. Whatever the connection, Frank Lloyd
Wright was a master of the style and
executed it with great drama.

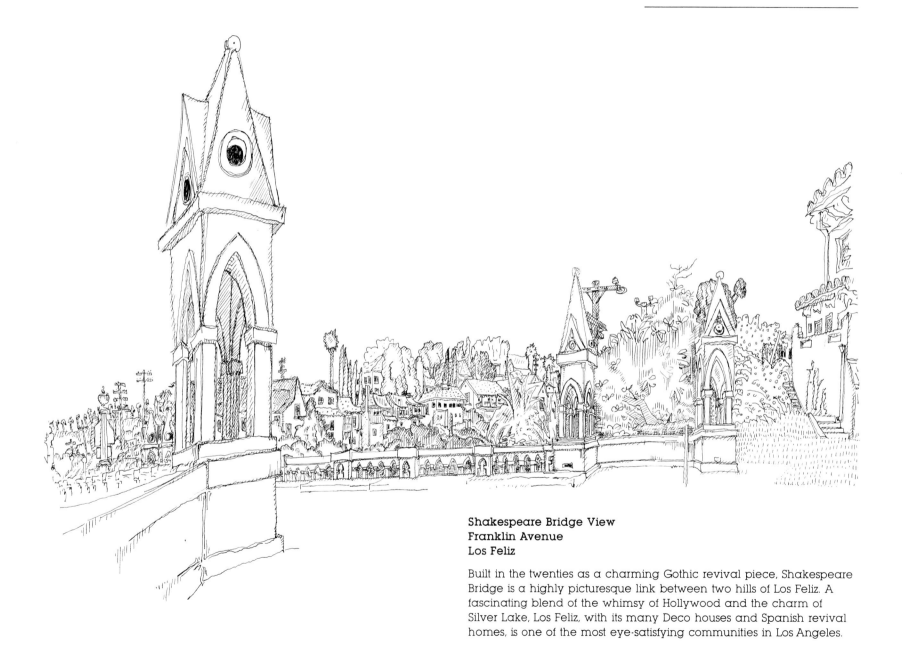

**Shakespeare Bridge View**
**Franklin Avenue**
**Los Feliz**

Built in the twenties as a charming Gothic revival piece, Shakespeare Bridge is a highly picturesque link between two hills of Los Feliz. A fascinating blend of the whimsy of Hollywood and the charm of Silver Lake, Los Feliz, with its many Deco houses and Spanish revival homes, is one of the most eye-satisfying communities in Los Angeles.

**View into Silver Lake
Sunset and Mayview Drives
Los Feliz**

**The Griffith Observatory
Top of Vermont Avenue
Los Feliz**

The Griffith Observatory and Planetarium plays host to more nationalities than there are constellations in the sky. You can hear a galaxy of languages; you can see a dazzling display of colorful costumes. I noticed a surly motorcycle boy chatting with Pakistanis wrapped in gauze. That's L.A.

Designed by John C. Austin and F.M. Ashley, the Observatory was constructed in 1935. It's a *moderne* delight, a brooch set on the crest of a hill in Griffith Park. In the evening, the Observatory grins down at L.A. like a Cheshire cat in on a cosmic joke.

ORANGE
COUNTY

**The Norwalk Square Sign**
**Pioneer and Telegraph**
**Norwalk**

This huge sign sits on top of a chicken restaurant, at the junction of streets called "Pioneer" and "Telegraph." The restaurant and the street names suggest our Western heritage. Perhaps the sign does too—a remembrance of carnivals past. It is a delight of lights running up from the restaurant roof to a grandiose "Norwalk Square" in the sky. And if that's not festive enough—there's a tent of lights arching even higher. Norwalk will not be ignored.

**Disneyland** (*overleaf*)
**1313 South Harbor Boulevard**
**Anaheim**

L.A.'s main industry is amusement. Disneyland, the greatest amusement center of all, began in 1955. Its mock Matterhorn, a famous smog-shrouded beacon, guides pleasure seekers to their utopia. Sleeping Beauty's Castle is the appropriate symbol for acres of phantasmagorical delights.

My favorite amusement is the marching band that parades down the main thoroughfare every hour or so. The drum major is a mechanical toy come to life. Big apple cheeks and a proud, puffed-out stomach.

Everyone knows about Disneyland. And, with the exception of a lost child or two, everyone is happy there.

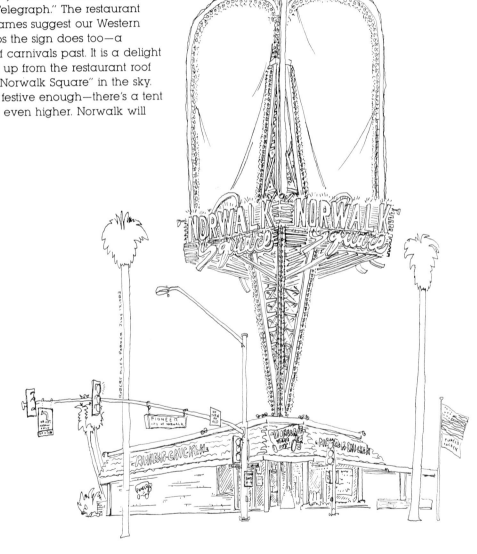

**Knott's Berry Farm—Ghost Town:
Goldie's Place
8039 Beach Boulevard
Buena Park**

Buena Park's claim to fame is that it's loaded with tourist entertainment: the Movieland Wax Museum, the Palace of the Dancing Stallions, and Knott's Berry Farm, to name a few.

The Knotts were a genuine pioneer family. They came over the mountains in a covered wagon. The story continued—the family matriarch turned berries into pies and then added chicken dinners... and in the end there was Knott's Berry Farm. You can sense a sincerity behind this Western saga that, for me, makes Knott's Berry Farm the most pleasant and down-to-earth of all the entertainment centers in Southern California. It's hokey and genuine at the same time.

The Old Trails Hotel was the first building rescued by the Knott family. Appropriately, it was built the same year the Knotts came to California—1868. The hotel was the antecedent for a whole town of relics, most of which were about to rot and decay on their original sites. Many of the buildings are "real," and then again many of them aren't. The Assay House, for example, was built in 1940.

Goldie's Place was copied after an old building in Bodie. Though the Knotts are fine, upstanding people, they knew no frontier ghost town would be complete without a house of ill repute.

**Knott's Berry Farm—Ghost Town:
The Assay Office and the Old Trails Hotel
Buena Park**

### John Barcelo's Challenge Dairy
### 13017 South Street
### Cerritos

This building is a remnant of a once-upon-a-time Orange County—a place of vast fields and bountiful harvests, of dairy farms and berry patches. With few exceptions, that's all gone now.

### The Alpha Beta Market
### Beach Boulevard Shopping Center
### Stanton

Supermarkets have a history too.

Albert Gerard was the proud owner of the Triangle Cash Market. In 1917, he changed his store's concept to one of self-service. He arranged the goods alphabetically on the shelves. Hence, the Alpha Beta.

This supermarket grabs the passerby without his ever really noticing it. Tall palms point to that equally tall Alpha Beta sign. The long, low structure planted in an asphalt field beckons, promising rows and rows of supplies—and goodies. In its own functional way, this is the best-looking building in Stanton.

### The Fullerton Train Station
### Transportation Complex
### Fullerton

Fullerton is east of the Santa Ana Freeway and north of the Riverside Freeway. (In Orange County everything is defined by the highway grid.) To the west of the Santa Ana, Orange County towns are chock-full of plastic and neon, cars and people. Fullerton is not quite that way. For the most part, the place is fresh and sparkly. Its citizens have a healthy glow. Everything's so spiffy, they renovate last year's malls.

In 1887, Ed Amerige drove a stake into the mustard fields, and Fullerton began. Before that, the town had been part of Rancho San Juan Cajon de Santa Ana, owned by Juan Pacifico Ontiveras. In 1904, Fullerton was incorporated. The community's mainstays were Valencia oranges, walnuts, avocados, and vegetables. (Now the principal product seems to be fresh-cheeked children.) All that produce had to reach market—and that's where Mr. Fullerton came in. He brought the train to town.

Construction of the Union Pacific Station began in the early 1900s, was halted for World War I, and was completed in 1922. It's a haunting, even unsettling example of mission revival style, topped with an intrusion of zigzag *moderne*. The old station now sits on pilings—it's been moved from somewhere down the line. It's waiting to become part of a trendy new Transportation Center.

THE FULLERTON TRAIN STATION · JANUARY 19, 1983
ROBERT MILES PARKER

### The Melody Inn
### Harbor Boulevard
### Fullerton

It's the Melody Inn, Fullerton's oldest bar—a bit of vernacular architecture, the everyday sort of buildings that are so common and comfortable you hardly notice them. Inside the Melody Inn things are common too. The patrons are young and Fullerton-hip. They affect a smart-ass bravado and let their filter-tip cigarettes dangle below baby-face eyes. Toughies with the Amway touch.

### Pat Diamond's House
### 221 Whiting Street
### Fullerton

Orange County is full of cottage revival architecture—little machines for comfortable living.

### Vietnamese Area
### Bolsa Avenue
### Westminster

A few Vietnamese families happened to settle in Westminster in the mid-seventies. And Vietnamese have been coming ever since. The culture they've created is in transition between Saigon and Los Angeles. On Bolsa Avenue, the Vietnamese have taken typical shopping center structures and orientalized them.

Los Angeles has always been a haven for people from other places. The diversity of L.A. personifies the American dream—it's a city of refuge, a city where hope is reborn.

**The Red Cross House** *(left)*
**418 North West Street**
**Anaheim**

In the great schmear of Orange County, every now and then you stumble on a joyous discovery—like this building. The Red Cross has its headquarters here. They've polished the Queen Anne tower, shingles, and spindles till they sparkle. You're not sure if it's reality or a Disney illusion.

**The Oldest House in Anaheim** *(above)*
**West Street**
**Anaheim**

This is said to be the oldest house in Anaheim, but it looks as if it knew Disneyland would not be far behind. That spiny back belongs on a Disney dinosaur.

Anaheim was settled in 1857 by middle-class San Francisco Germans. It remained, until the booming forties, a pleasant agricultural town. There are few remnants of such pastoral pleasures now.

**The McCoy-Hare House** *(right)*
**341 Hazard Street**
**Westminster**

The McCoy-Hare House is a wistful symbol of a lost past. It was built in the early 1870s and served as a drugstore. The doll-like board and batten was constructed by Westminster's first doctor, James McCoy. Later the little building was the home of Marie Hare, a local educator. She lived there from 1912 until 1974. Then, in 1976, it was restored and set on its current postage-stamp plot.

Westminster was established as a Presbyterian colony. Anaheim, in kindred manner, was settled by staid Germans. It was from such roots that Orange County conservatism grew.

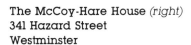

**The Anaheim Convention Center** *(right)*
**Katella Street**
**Anaheim**

After looking at all of L.A., I have decided
that Anaheim has some rather special
architecture. Many of L.A.'s towns are bland,
but not Anaheim. Those motels are so brazen
in their gaudy dress, they're fun. And the
Convention Center is an honest workman's
patch in the crazy quilt of Anaheim's
architecture. The dome in its harness sweeps
cleanly and easily, and it is set off nicely by
the sky-jabbing arch. Del E. Webb's (1965)
design is an eye-pleasing solution to getting
a bunch of people together under one roof.

**"The Bear Tree" in Hobby City** *(left)*
**1240 South Beach Boulevard**
**Anaheim**

For days I wandered the County, searching for unique architecture.
I felt I was drowning in a sea of look-alike houses and garden
apartments. Even shopping centers and gas stations began to look
refreshing. And then I found "The Bear Tree."

It's a new building, completed just this past year. Michelle and
Jason Walker run the "Tree" and live upstairs. It's just stuffed with
teddy bears: cute cuddly ones, big fat ones... ever so many
charming teddy bears.

The family designed and constructed this tree because they
"couldn't find anyone else who knew how." That's hardly surprising.

**The Crystal Cathedral**
**12141 Lewis Street**
**Garden Grove**

If a brand-new church can be said to be holy, then the Crystal Cathedral is. The latticework grid is inspired. And the soaring interior space is ethereal. The "glass curtain" walls demand respect, maybe awe.

It really is a cathedral—so many people pulled together to create it. You can feel that. You can feel millions of everyday folks who, together, have made something beyond themselves. Like its medieval counterparts, the Crystal Cathedral is the most glorious creation in the community. The masses come here to this sacred place to have their lives realized—there's nothing else in Garden Grove that can make them so special.

The history of the Cathedral, completed in 1980, is almost folklore. The concept was born in an Orange drive-in movie theater in 1955. The world-famous architect, Philip Johnson, was commissioned to create this symbol of majesty in a suburban landscape normally associated with mediocrity. And the small contributions of many plain folks helped bring the project to fruition.

**The Nixon Birthplace** (*above*)
18061 Yorba Linda Boulevard
Yorba Linda

Yorba Linda is another lovely Orange County suburban town. It's rolling hills and pretty tract houses. But in Yorba Linda the tract houses are stucco smart, they're big and tan, and they have chimneys—maybe two or three chimneys. Every street's a boulevard, and even the shopping centers are inviting.

I always look for architecture that tells me how a place came to be the place it is. Usually, I find it in the town center. But this town center has been altered till it looks like a friendly but noncommittal shopping mall.

Right next door to the shopping mall/town center is a little knoll of unfriendliness. On top of that knoll sits a rather ordinary Craftsman style house. Frank Nixon built that house in 1912. His son, Richard Nixon, was born there in 1913. You reach the structure by a dirt road, where you are uninvited at the entrance gate: "Occupied, do not disturb." An erstwhile telephone booth announces itself as a guest register, but with no register book. The shrubs and the trees have a menacing, grabbing look. It's really not like Yorba Linda at all. But it is a shrine to something very American.

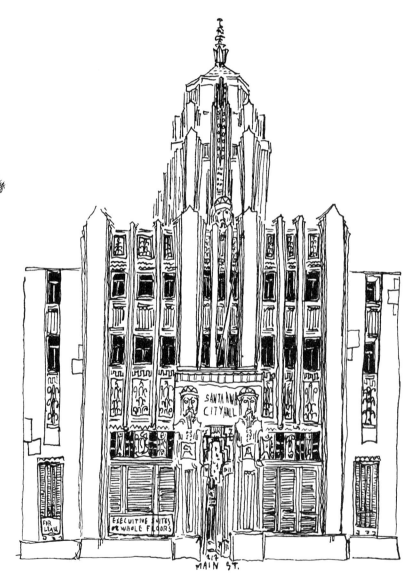

**Santa Ana City Hall** *(left)*
**217 Main Street**
**Santa Ana**

Every Southern Californian knows the name
Santa Ana. After all, it may be the busiest
freeway there is. But guess what? There's a
town too. It's stuck down near the bottom of
greater Los Angeles and is the county seat
for Orange County. Santa Ana has real
touches of style. Even though surrounded by
the uninteresting results of the building boom
that began in the fifties, Santa Ana has
retained much of its downtown core. And it's
proud. You can feel the pride in Austin and
Wildman's 1934 City Hall—a small town reply
to the city hall of big L.A. Soaring pinnacles
and scowling Deco faces make the *moderne*
structure a classic.

**The 302 Cafe, the La Gloria, and the West Coast Theater**
**Main Street and Third West**
**Santa Ana**

Further samplings of the delightful Santa Ana downtown can be
found in the now deserted 302 Cafe and the ornate West Coast
Theater. The theater serves the large Mexican-American population
that has reclaimed Santa Ana for its own.

Santa Ana has used urban redevelopment funds to its advantage.
Where other towns have destroyed their urban centers to create cute
office parks and ugly parking facilities, this town has doggedly
protected its original cityscape. Even the new parking garage is
designed as an attractive adjunct to the real downtown.

**The Antioch Baptist Church** (*below*)
**Corner of Orange Street**
**and Almond Avenue**
**Orange**

A real surprise, the town of Orange. There's still a pleasant village atmosphere about it, and it even has its original central plaza. The trees and palms look as if they've been there since the town was plotted in 1870. The rest of Orange is part of the L.A. blur, but its heart is a rewarding respite—with architectural charms like the Antioch Baptist Church.

THE ANTIOCH BAPTIST CHURCH · CORNER OF ORANGE STREET
AND ALMOND AVENUE · ROBERT MILES PARKER · JUNE 14, 1983
IN ORANGE

**The Stevens House** (*above*)
**228 Main Street**
**Tustin**

Tustin people are probably glad their town never grew. They should be. The community is a rather pleasant counterbalance to the busyness of Orange County. The Sherman Stevens House (1887) is a perfect example of the quietude and comfort that Tustin retains. The home remained in the Stevens family until 1980 and is now part of Stevens Square. The design is primarily the work of Douglas Gfeller. The Square is a complex of apartments and offices, a good example of thoughtful development centered around one original building.

# PASADENA
# AND THE
# SAN GABRIEL
# VALLEY

'79
S RAYMOND AVE
ROBERT MILES PARKER
CASTLE GREEN
PASADENA
FEBRUAT
MARCH 9, 1983

**The Castle Green** (overleaf)
**99 South Raymond**
**Pasadena**

The San Gabriel Valley towns were created by railroad interests, who built their lines way out to Cucamonga and such places. And then they built outlandish hotels so that people could ride the trains to an adventurous destination. It's hard to imagine a more outlandish place to spend a night than the Castle Green.

Although it's an apartment house now, the Castle Green still glows with all that is magic in Pasadena. It smolders amid dank and romantic vegetation. The castle itself is dung-colored cement complemented by red tiled, Moorish roofs. Romantic Spanish balconies lace the walls—you feel the presence of mantillaed ladies peering out at you.

The castle was designed by Frederick Roehrig at the turn of the century to complement his earlier hotel across the street. The front protrusion appears to be all that's left of what was "The Bridge of Sighs," which connected the two. Only remnants of the earlier (1880s) hotel are left. Both it and the castle were the dream of patent-medicine magnate Colonel G.G. Green. He hoped to cash in on the great late-eighties boom—and left us this.

**The Three Signs**
**Corner of Foothill Boulevard**
**and White Avenue**
**Pomona**

Signs can be more attractive than the buildings around them.

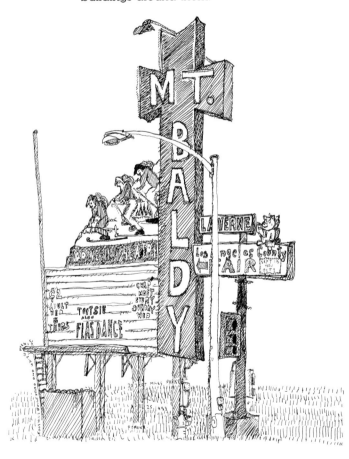

**The Seventh-Day Adventist Church** (*above*)
**Corner of Third and Gordon**
**Pomona**

Pomona is one of the largest cities in all of Los Angeles. It is also one of the most tragic. The smog is dreadful, and probably much of that pollution comes directly from Pomona factories. The city has a chopped-up look and jumps from one working-class neighborhood to another.

Pomona does boast a mall, which is one of the loneliest, most unattractive places I've ever walked. Hollow muzak ricochets off the vacant buildings. But Pomona also has lots of fun architecture, much of it dating from the 1880s, when the town was founded. The Seventh-Day Adventist Church was designed in 1895 by F. Davis, who left us a charming Pomona building.

**Scripps College View** (*below*)
**Claremont**

Claremont is truly a town apart. It has an aura quite different from any other city in greater L.A. Small wonder. The town was created by Easterners who wanted to live in an environment not unlike the one they had left behind. They even brought their own trees—there are probably more varieties of trees in Claremont than in any other city in Southern California. The town's architecture, too, has an Eastern flavor—it looks like Main Street, Vermont. Claremont is a comfortable, complacent, ivory-tower sort of place.

The first of the Claremont Colleges was established in Pomona (1887). Claremont built a huge hotel, and then the famous bust came. Pomona College was invited to fill the hotel, and the city has since grown into a community of colleges. There is Scripps (1926), "a center for serenity and reflection"; Claremont McKenna (1947); the science and engineering oriented Harvey Mudd (1955); and, most recently, Pitzer (1963). There are also other university centers and the Claremont Graduate School. Claremont is a haven for the rarified academic experience.

The Scripps College campus personifies Claremont. It was designed in the Mediterranean style, popular in the Southwest during the twenties and thirties. It is a lovely assemblage of courtyards, loggias, terraces, and gardens—all enhanced by the gentle, understated style.

**The Pitzer House** *(above)*
**Baseline and Towne**
**Claremont**

The Pitzer House (circa 1910, Robert H. Orr, architect) was the home of the founder of Pitzer College. It is a perfect example of an architecture that reflects its environment. The house, cool and comfortable, is constructed of arroyo stone, in a style found all over Los Angeles. Sometimes a porch, sometimes a wall, sometimes just the fireplace is done in fieldstone. The effect is always humane and charming.

**The Shrimp House**
**Foothill Boulevard**
**Claremont**

Imagine, this boat sits at least fifty miles from the ocean: a restaurant stranded in the great Los Angeles desert.

**The San Dimas Hotel** *(right)*
**First and San Dimas**
**San Dimas**

In 1885, the Santa Fe completed its tracks between L.A. and San Bernardino. The San Jose Ranch Company, in cahoots with the railroads, built the town of San Dimas—the halfway point. As always, part of creating a town was building a giant hotel. The San Dimas Hotel is one of the few such left.

It was designed by Joseph Cather Newsom and was completed in 1887. The redwood for the building was floated on rafts from Northern California to San Pedro, then hauled inland. But the hotel never had a chance to be a hotel. By the time it was completed, the great land boom was a bust, and this giant structure became a private home.

The San Dimas Hotel is no grand piece of architecture, but it is L.A. history.

**The Water Plant**
**Gladstone Street and Moreno Avenue**
**La Verne**

La Verne (established 1888) is another Santa
Fe railroad station town. Perhaps its greatest
distinction is its Spanish-revival water
purification plant (Daniel A. Elliot, 1940). It's
reassuring to know that the water gets
cleaned up in style in La Verne.

**Old Church** *(right)*
**Irwindale Avenue and Juarez Street**
**Irwindale**

Irwindale is not the sort of town that gets a nod from architecture books. In its way, though, it is glorious. Irwindale seems to be the great divide—it separates the smart San Gabriel Valley towns like Pasadena from the bedroom communities of Azusa and Glendora.

Gigantic construction machinery looms ominously. Gravel-pit machines gnaw at the San Gabriel Mountains. At night the erector-set monsters twinkle with lonely little lights echoing each other as they dance up and down the strange gargantuan forms.

The town has something like 700 people—that's all. It has practically no architecture of note, and very few houses. There are simply lots of industrial plants. I don't know how this charming little church managed to be born, nor how it manages to survive. Maybe it's because its Craftsman style shingle and rock construction suggests the mountain-eating machines. The church has no name, no times listed for meetings and services. Like the machines, it's anonymous.

**The Azusa Train Station**
**Santa Fe Street**
**Azusa**

Remember Mel Blanc on the "Jack Benny Program"?—"All aboard for Anaheim, Azusa, and Cuc—amonga!"

Who would ever have guessed that this is what the Azusa train station looks like?

**The Donut Hole** (*below*)
**Hacienda Boulevard and Elliott Avenue**
**La Puente**

La Puente is just another place in a sea of other places. It's basic L.A. strip development—tract houses, commercial buildings, little that's interesting, nothing that's unique. It's what the world assumes Los Angeles is. But there's more to L.A. than this. Great secrets are hidden all about—and the Donut Hole is surely one of them.

Look-alike La Puente becomes a special place as you head down Donut Lane. Where else but in L.A. would you drive through a donut? When you enter the Donut Hole, for a split second you're in another world—everything becomes a glazed glory. Then it's out the other end and back to just plain life.

**Glendora City Hall** (*above*)
**Glendora and Foothill**
**Glendora**

Glendora: comfortable; pleasant; new tract houses on the edge of the mountains; older tract houses down by the center of town. And this charming little Mediterranean-revival town hall.

**Workman Cemetery and Mausoleum**
**Industry Historic Park**
**Industry**

It always fascinates me to hear of a city named Industry. And how nice that it's near a city named Commerce.

Industry is hard to understand. It's an old town, boasting a couple of original adobes, but it's mostly factories. I did discover, however, the Walter P. Temple Memorial. What a pleasure to find a Greek revival building in a town called Industry. California's last Mexican governor, Pio Pico, is buried here. That, too, adds a touch of historical charm.

**The Rotary Air Compressor Building**
**13419 Valley Boulevard**
**Bassett**

As the towns slide southward from the San Gabriel Mountains, they get meaner. In Bassett you encounter lots of the ubiquitous Los Angeles lowriders. Shiny Fords and sleek Chevrolets have their bodies raised way above the ground, or lowered so that they slink down right next to the asphalt. Macho is the image, even for air compressors.

APRIL 25, 1983 · CORNER OF CENTRAL AND BUENA VISTA STREETS          ROBERT MILES PARKER

**The Duarte School**
**Central Street and Buena Vista Street**
**Duarte**

The mission revival Duarte School was constructed in 1908. Its
designer was F.S. Allen. They say the town of Duarte once had many
special structures. But there are not many of them left now. And the
Duarte School is threatened too. You see, it's not "earthquake proof."
But the mayor thinks the school is "pretty nice and we should kind of
save it."

**The Aztec Hotel**
**311 Foothill Boulevard**
**Monrovia**

The Aztec Hotel is the most audacious structure in Monrovia—reason enough to see the town. Constructed in 1925, it still delights or perhaps perplexes everyone who walks by. The building was designed by Robert Stacy-Judd and is the embodiment of one man's philosophy. He felt the need to find the "true American style." To him this was it. It seems he was perplexed too. He named his dream "The Aztec," yet the style is Mayan.

The Aztec's lobby is every bit as peculiar as its facade. Original murals painted by Stacy-Judd are now veneered with the stain of tobacco smoke, while gnarled old men who seem to have crawled off the outside walls creep around the lobby.

The building is still the pride of Monrovia. The day I was there, a wedding reception was in progress. Innocent young people ogled the "Central American" wall murals, while the Aztec Room's Saturday selection of drinkers toasted the venerable building. Yes, Monrovia loves its old hotel. So did its architect. He hung a sign inside: "This Building, including all exterior and interior Ornament, Decorations, Mural Paintings, and Electrical Fixtures designed by Robert B. Stacy-Judd, architect, 1925."

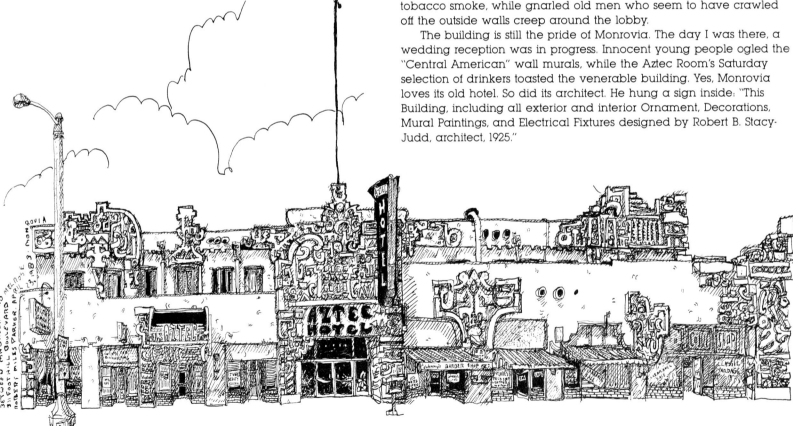

## The Santa Anita Race Track
**285 West Huntington**
**Arcadia**

Horse racing has been part of Arcadia for over a hundred years. First it was the silver dons, back in the days of Rancho Santa Anita. Then E.J. Lucky Baldwin bought the place and quickly became a racing enthusiast. And now the Santa Anita Race Track carries on the tradition.

In 1933, the Los Angeles Turf Club was organized on part of Baldwin's Santa Anita estate. Gordon B. Kaufmann was commissioned to design the Santa Anita Race Track. There's nothing like it anywhere else in Los Angeles. The structure is a fitting arena for the sport of kings. Even the great palms suggest the majesty and excitement of the race. The blue-green buildings are famous for their delicate frieze of golden horses. The towers, canopied walks, and latticework balconies suggest Fitzgerald characters in white flannels, cheering on their favorite thoroughbred. Even off-season, a stroll through the grounds can evoke thrilling memories of the trumpet blast and a throaty announcer: "... and they're off!"

**Mission San Gabriel** (*below*)
**537 West Mission Drive**
**San Gabriel**

Here's where it all started—where Los Angeles began. In what is now a suburban town, Mission San Gabriel was planted in 1771. Imagine a valley, a peaceful valley, with Indians (of whom six thousand are buried in the courtyard), oak trees spotting the hills, and silver dons escorting their mantilla-draped ladies. It was not until after the Civil War that the hordes of gringos began pouring in.

The church is beautiful and imbued with a sense of sanctity. It has that heavy incense-laden air you expect in an ancient place of worship. The adobe exterior is punctuated by buttresses. At one end is the old campanile; at the other is a stairway leading to the choir loft inside. The mission continues to fulfill its original purpose—it now ministers to newly settled Asians.

**The Pinney House** (*above*)
**225 North Lima Street**
**Sierra Madre**

Sierra Madre marks the end of Pasadena and the beginning of the towns that sidle on out the San Gabriel Valley. It sits on the edge of the San Gabriel Mountains at the foot of Mount Wilson and was originally a haven for people from the Midwest with health problems. Many of them came to the Pinney House, which, in 1886, was a smart hotel. The days may have been heavy with dripping mountain dew, but the roar of good health apparently returned to the guests. Perhaps that's the reason the architects, Samuel and Joseph Newsom, designed lion's faces under the swan-necked pediment of the front entrance.

**The Ocean Seafood Restaurant** (*below*)
**Garfield and Valley**
**Alhambra**

Alhambra (1873) is one of the oldest suburbs of Los Angeles. Benjamin Wilson, who created the town, intended to give it an exotic air. The streets have names I wouldn't dare try to pronounce, but the town was always pleasant and Anglo—never very exotic. But times change, and Alhambra is now at least twenty percent Chinese. A little exotic at last.

The Ocean Seafood Restaurant was constructed, I'm told, in 1938 as the Greyhound Station. It has seen use as a real estate office, a gas station, a chowder house, and, now, a Chinese restaurant.

**The Huntington Library** (*above*)
**1151 Oxford Road**
**San Marino**

Henry Huntington first visited the San Marino area in 1892 and purchased a ranch there in 1902, renaming it San Marino. From the time he bought the ranch, his idea was to share with the public both his land and the collection of books and art he had begun.

Huntington asked Myron Hunt and Elmer Grey to design his home (1910). He and his wife, Arabella, knew that someday their residence would become a public monument.

The gallery is academically neoclassic, with an impressive loggia and grand staircase at the front entrance. The art collection inside is more impressive still. Gainsborough's *Blue Boy* is on one side of the main gallery, facing Lawrence's *Pinky* on the other. And at the end of the same room is Reynolds's *Mrs. Siddons as the Tragic Muse*.

What splendid gifts Henry Huntington left to L.A.

## Andrianna's View
## Arroyo Boulevard
## Pasadena

Of all the Los Angeles cities, only Pasadena offers such a breathtaking view of freeways and streets. The Colorado Bridge (1913), latticed with arches and lined with lamps and wrought iron railing, is framed here by the 1968 Ventura Freeway. Winding through the valley is the footpathlike road, the Arroyo. And peeping through the distance is the tower of the old Vista del Arroyo Hotel, which will soon be used by the U.S. Court of Appeals.

## The Pacific Asia Museum (right)
## 46 North Los Robles Avenue
## Pasadena

Pasadena began as a cultural center. People came from all over the East and the Midwest to luxuriate under the lovely palms and take in the orange-blossom breezes. They built marvelous houses and glorious boulevards. They created a spectacular place. And then, it seems, they lost heart. Oh, some of it's still there—here and there. But so much is gone. The integrity of the center city was destroyed by the Ernest Hahn shopping complex, an absurd box with blank walls facing the street and every now and then a cookie-cutter hole for decoration.

Grace Nicholson had this museum constructed in 1924. The architects were Marston, Van Pelt, and Maybury. The idea was to display Miss Nicholson's Oriental art collection and at the same time to give her a cozy little place to live. The museum is in the Imperial Palace style. There are Chinese dog finials with absurd Pekinese mugs, marvelous green tiles, and stone carvings—all imported from China, of course.

Grace Nicholson created something special for her city. She left a fine legacy: a distinct work of art in a growing sea of anonymity.

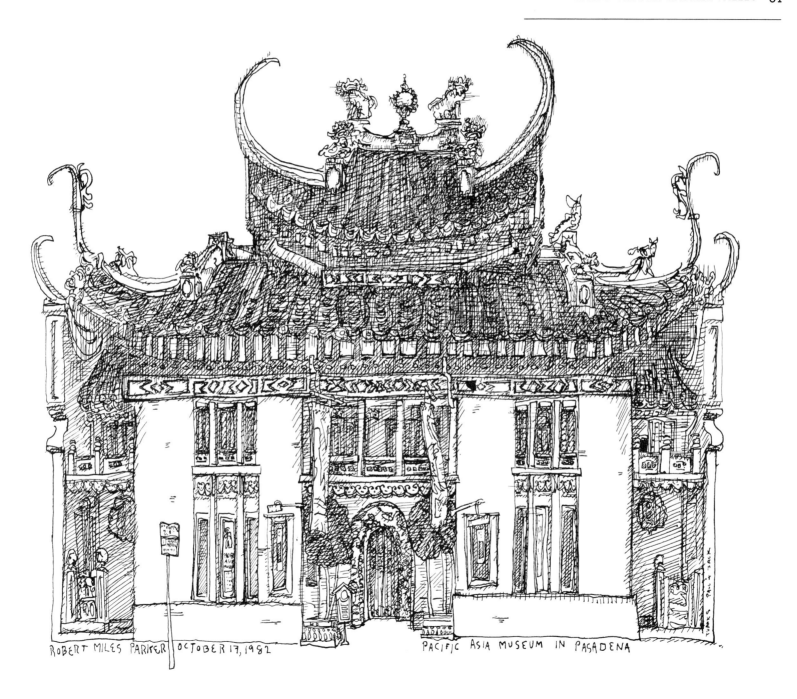

ROBERT MILES PARKER  OCTOBER 17, 1982          PACIFIC ASIA MUSEUM IN PASADENA

**Le Chateau
34 Mentor Avenue
Pasadena**

Pasadena must have been full of old people from the start. They're everywhere now: down the block at Beadle's Cafeteria, across the street in a retirement hotel, and filling Le Chateau. Some doddering and grim, some lost in private worlds, still others starched and haughty.

The elderly ladies have a good time gossiping. The elderly gentlemen, too. But put them together and there's surly silence.

This was once a very classy neighborhood. But now Le Chateau, with its fifty-one units, is tucked between two parking lots. In the best Pasadena tradition, it remains manicured and elaborately coiffed.

The manageress proudly confided that Le Chateau has steam heat. An original Otis elevator, too!

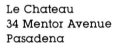

## Bullock's Pasadena
## 401 South Lake Avenue
## Pasadena

Lake Avenue Bullock's was popular the day it opened its doors in the fall of 1947, and it's just as popular now—thumbing its nose at upstart shopping malls like the Ernie Hahn blob in downtown Pasadena.

The streamline *moderne* structure was designed by Wilton Wurdeman and Welton Becket. The atmosphere is similar, though in an updated way, to Bullock's Wilshire (the chain's "Specialty Store"). It has a French feeling—late *moderne* curves and a generous use of open space.

## The Gamble House
## 4 Westmoreland Place
## Pasadena

The Craftsman movement was a reaction against the mad exuberance of the Victorians. In many ways its buildings are the epitome of Southern California architecture. Its use of long and low Oriental forms can be traced back to the Japanese exhibit at the World's Columbian Exposition of 1893 in Chicago, while the half-timbered dwellings of the English countryside and the heavy-eaved houses of the Alps are still other influences behind the movement.

Charles and Henry Greene were the masters of the Craftsman style, and their masterpiece, the Gamble House (1908), sits in Pasadena. Each element of the structure—each piece of furniture, each lighting fixture, each rug—is designed to relate aesthetically to the whole. The effect is one of almost overwhelming artistic integrity.

**The Rose Bowl**
**Brookside Park**
**Pasadena**

**Peter Adams's House**
**485 Maylin Avenue**
**Pasadena**

Every house has a history. This typical overgrown Pasadena place is no exception. The architect was Frederick Roehrig, the same fellow who designed the outrageous Castle Green. He constructed this home in 1894. The original owner, Mr. May, founded a bank that later became a part of the great Security Pacific.

And that was only the beginning. Julie McDonald lived at 485 Maylin for a long time. This 6'1" sculptress, who used a jack hammer to hew out her work, kept a veritable African menagerie. She was the author of *Almost Human*, a book about a baboon, one of several she kept on the property. Other residents included, at various times, a jaguar, some hyenas, and the perennial nine cats. Julie loved people, too. It is rumored that Julie McDonald had an ongoing affair with jazzman Charlie Parker.

Pasadena isn't quite as proper as you may have heard.

# GLENDALE
# AND THE
# VALLEY

FOREST LAWN
GLENDALE.
ROBERT
MILES
PARKER
AUGUST 20 1983

**Forest Lawn** (*overleaf*)
**1712 South Glendale Avenue**
**Glendale**

Forest Lawn was founded by Dr. Hubert L. Eaton. Fredrick Hansen was his landscape architect. Dr. Eaton, in 1917, envisioned his cemetery as "a great park, devoid of misshapen monuments... where lovers new and old shall love to stroll." What he created is a marvelous "view of Toledo." Perched on a hillside near the Glendale city limits, Forest Lawn has become a world-renowned Mecca. Jean Harlow, W.C. Fields, and Tom Mix rest in peace at Forest Lawn. I've heard that Aimee Semple McPherson is there too, and that she has a telephone inside her crypt.

The collection of kitsch art at Forest Lawn is as amazing as it is typically L.A. There is a stained glass re-creation of Leonardo's *Last Supper* and the tombs of the seven "Immortals"—including Carrie Jacobs Bond, the composer of "I Love You Truly," Gutzon Borglum, who carved Mt. Rushmore, and Dr. Eaton himself.

Forest Lawn is, perhaps, a sentinel for the Valley, a place where history and traditions were buried long ago and where sentimental smarm lives on.

**Gary's View of North Hollywood**
**5664 Ensign Avenue**
**North Hollywood**

The great San Fernando Valley was originally wheat fields and orchards, but they were swept away as land-hungry Los Angeles moved in to take possession. These fields and orchards needed water, and L.A. had the water. Only by allowing themselves to be annexed to the city could the Valley's communities exist at all.

There are almost no distinctive buildings in the Valley. Development came too late and too fast—in the fifties and sixties. By then people were in too big a hurry to care about monuments.

North Hollywood is just another place: a backyard view, a shack, a flat-faced apartment building, some strange desert plants.

**The Warner Brothers Building** (*below*)
**Olive and Kenwood**
**Burbank**

The $14 million Warner Brothers office building was completed in 1981. It was designed by the Luckman Partnership, with an unusual interior-wall system created in collaboration with the firm of Milton I. Swimmer, Planning and Design, Inc. Production companies need fluctuating space: a film production often begins with a small staff, increases to a larger staff, and then decreases again as the work winds down. So the unique wall system of this building allows interior spaces to be varied with that need in mind. That space variation is reflected in the almost mobile effect of the building's exterior.

**The Edmund House** (*above*)
**13956 Magnolia**
**Sherman Oaks**

"Back in the old days, there were special post offices out here—there were really little towns. Now they all run together," remembers Mrs. Edmund. At that time movie stars lived in places like Sherman Oaks and Encino. Some still do. It's cooler in these towns. Safer too. The communities are stable, comfortable, and faceless.

The Edmund House was constructed in 1938. The style is Monterey revival—pre-tract and definitely blessed with a face.

**The Good Knight Inn** (*right*)
**9247 Sepulveda Boulevard**
**Sepulveda**

Just what the Valley needs, some Orange County architecture. Well, it's better than another tract house. The Good Knight Inn was constructed around 1960 and is currently owned by Mark Chen.

**Mission San Fernando**
**15151 San Fernando Mission Boulevard**
**Mission Hills**

The San Fernando Mission was founded in 1797. The mission church was destroyed in the great earthquake of 1971 and has been replaced by an exact replica. Even the replacement has a haunting, sacred feeling.

The convento (monastery) building is the signature place of the San Fernando Mission, one of the loveliest structures in all the Valley. It was begun in 1810 and completed a dozen years later. The convento originally contained over twenty different rooms, including quarters for two priests and guest accommodations. The front wall is supported by twenty-one Romanesque arches, creating a serene portico running the length of the monastery.

**Our Lady of Peace Church** (*below*)
**Nordhoff Street**
**Sepulveda**

Not far from the old mission sits Our Lady of Peace. Roman Catholicism has traveled a strange path. When I asked the curate to tell me the story of his church—when it was built, what the style is, how large the congregation is—he curtly replied that he had no time.

**The Diner** (*above*)
**18448 Saticoy**
**Northridge**

Can you believe that this is a subtle and rather charming complex of signs and buildings? Well, it is, compared to everything else in Northridge. It might even be termed unique.

The Diner was constructed about 1940, a few years after Carl S. Dentzel, a local citizen, decided to rename the community. He felt that a "more respectable" name was in order. Too bad he made that decision. Between 1908 and 1935, Northridge had been known as Zelzah. Isn't that just like the Valley—making everything original and charming into something "respectable."

**The Leonis Adobe** (*above*)
**23537 Calabasas Road**
**Calabasas**

Fortunately, Calabasas has kept its charming name, but that's about all. The rest of it is Valley-artsy—and freeway, of course. The Leonis Adobe is squeezed in between the freeway and "ye shoppes."

The community is one of the oldest settlements in the Valley. In the late 19th Century, it was a stagecoach stop on the road from San Francisco to Los Angeles. This adobe, which was the post house, was built around 1850. It's a lovely leftover from wild-west Valley days, though its architectural style is now very Monterey, with Queen Anne ornamentation. Miguel Leonis modernized the old stage stop when he moved there in the seventies. It hardly looks like an adobe any more—but that's how trendy the Valley is.

**Old Methodist Church** (*right*)
**Oakwood Memorial Park, Lassen Street**
**Chatsworth**

Chatsworth, too, was on the stagecoach route from San Francisco to L.A. But now it's just another Valley place. This little 1904 Methodist Church was rescued from the creeping conformity of the Valley. How? By being moved to a graveyard.

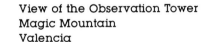

**View of the Observation Tower**
**Magic Mountain**
**Valencia**

**Entry to the Revolution Ride** (*above*)
**Magic Mountain**
**Valencia**

Six Flags Magic Mountain is the northernmost playland for Los
Angeles. It is situated in the breathtakingly beautiful Santa Susana
Mountains, at the northern boundary of the greater L.A. area. The
park attracts a different crowd from those who frequent the city's
other amusement areas. While Disneyland's visitors seem fresh and
antiseptic and Knott's Berry Farm's are folksy and down-home, the
people who frequent Six Flags seem more proletarian and less polite.
(There are signs everywhere prohibiting breaking into line,
threatening immediate expulsion from the park. They are ignored.)

Nevertheless, the park is a lot of fun. The rides are exciting. The
Revolution turns you upside down and inside out five times—at least
it feels that way. And the roller coaster, the Colossus, is one of the
most adventurous in the United States.

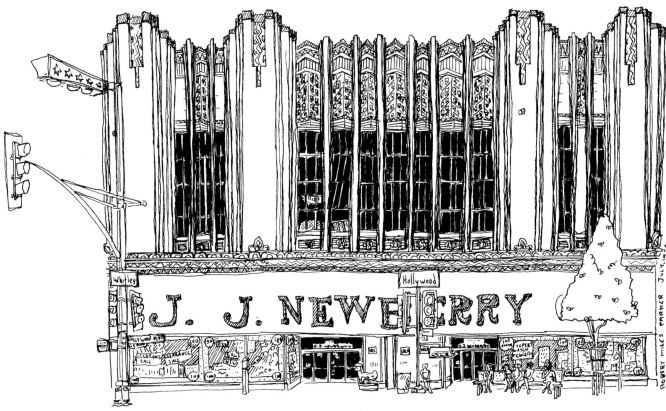

**Hollywood Tower** (*overleaf*)
**6200 Franklin Avenue**
**Hollywood**

Hollywood Tower epitomizes the hopes and
aspirations of those people who still pour into
town in search of tawdry riches and will-o'-
the-wisp fame. They lounge all about the
Tower, most of them as musty as the old
building. But musty though it may be,
Hollywood Tower is a landmark. It sits at a
bend in the Hollywood Freeway, a harbinger
of the dreamworld you're about to pass
through.

**J.J. Newberry**
**Hollywood Boulevard and Whitley**
**Hollywood**

This is probably as classy a piece of Hollywood as anyone would
want—the J.J. Newberry Store. Deco architecture is one of the
grander styles Los Angeles has embraced. The flash and glory of the
late twenties is smartly reflected in the gold, turquoise, and glazed
terra-cottas of this "five and dime." The architect? Apparently just part
of the Newberry staff.

    Like most of Hollywood Boulevard, this store is not much fun now.
The merchandise has a dusty feel. The customers look dusty, too. Stars
on the sidewalk and stars on the lamppost can't bring back the glory
that Newberry's so wistfully recalls.

**Frederick's of Hollywood** (*left*)
**6608 Hollywood Boulevard**
**Hollywood**

The Art Deco Frederick's is not the sleazy emporium it once was. The exterior is a little daring, in two or three shades of violet. But most of the merchandise now is middle-of-the-road. You can find garments quite the match for Frederick's wares in most basement lingerie sections of suburban department stores. How times have changed.

**The Janes House** (*below*)
**6541 Hollywood Boulevard**
**Hollywood**

The only surviving private home among the shops and shrines of the boulevard.

**The First Hollywood Studio
Hollywood and Vine
Hollywood**

In 1913, Cecil B. deMille, Samuel Goldwyn, and Jesse Lasky used half of this old barn to film *The Squaw Man*, the first feature-length motion picture made in Hollywood.

The structure has now been moved from this temporary Vine Street rest stop to a new home across from the Hollywood Bowl. It's to be a museum—a clapboard monument to the fantasy industry.

**The Garden Court Apartment Hotel** (*right*)
**7021 Hollywood Boulevard
Hollywood**

The Garden Court (1919), along with all its bemused caryatids, is quietly crumbling away. Built in neo-Renaissance style, the place sings a soft but tuneful swan song.

The song? A Hollywood chant—of magic, faded names, and verses that murmur the old show-biz story. The front steps are chipped and the lobby is a dusty and forgotten movie set. When you climb those steps and stand in the empty foyer, you can hear, "They wouldn't rent to show people in the twenties. Not till Louis B. Mayer lived in Number 417. The American School of Dance was here for twenty-nine years. Eugene Loring, you know. Mack Sennett lived here for thirty-eight years."

The once shiny windows are festooned with rags. But the hibiscus still bloom, and the invocation of great names continues. "Charlotte Boerner, Juliet Prowse, Cyd Charisse, Jane Fonda, Debbie Reynolds—they all took dance here. And, you know, there used to be tennis courts all the way down to the corner. Yes, we were very exclusive when Mack Sennett stayed here. Randy Quaid (*The Last Detail*—it got an award)—we helped him practice here at night, in the lobby." The names go on and on, each one conjured with a faded smile, each bouncing off dreary walls, and then lost. Rudolph Valentino, Marilyn Monroe, James Dean...

THE FIRST HOLLYWOOD STUDIO NOW SITTING ON VINE STREET ROBERT MILES PARKER · HOLLYWOOD · 9·12·82

SALE-LEASE

GARDEN COURT
APARTMENT HOTEL

ROBERT MILES PARKER · MARCH, 1977

HOLLYWOOD BOULEVARD, HOLLYWOOD, CALIFORNIA

**Paramount Studios—South Gate**
**Marathon Street at Bronson**
**Hollywood**

Paramount considers itself the star of
Hollywood studios. In fact, it's the only studio
left in Hollywood proper. The Mediterranean
facade and the old gates just hint at the
magic created inside. The tour buses still go
by, and the tourists click their cameras and
stare in awe. Too bad what they see is
crumbling.

**The Capitol Records Tower** (below)
**1750 Vine Street**
**Hollywood**

Los Angeles loves to create monuments to
the enterprise of the moment. Welton Becket
designed the Capitol Records Tower in 1954,
and it holds its own with some of the other
wildly absurd architecture in town. It's a stack
of records spinning in the Hollywood skyline.

**Mann's Chinese Theater** (left)
**Hollywood Boulevard**
**Hollywood**

The Chinese Theater (formerly Grauman's) is
truly a shrine for pilgrims. Tourists always
have to step in the cement footprints of the
famous who have achieved Hollywood's
version of immortality on the sidewalks in
front of the theater. The grand pseudo-
oriental architecture was conceived by
Meyer and Holler, and the theater was
constructed in 1927. In those days they really
knew how to show a movie fan a good time.

**Deco Building on Santa Monica**
**6424 Santa Monica Boulevard**
**Hollywood**

A charming Santa Monica Boulevard Deco
(late twenties), almost lost in the hustle of the
street. Perhaps you could call the style
Regency *moderne*.

**The Trianon** (*left*)
**1752 Serrano Avenue**
**Hollywood**

French Regency? Norman Revival? The 1930s Hollywood castles are
difficult to label. Many of the towered apartment buildings were
constructed at a time when people were happy to live in their
fantasies. And the movie industry had created a world in which
fantasy was the order of the day.

The Trianon is one of the most famous of the castles. It is said that
for a while Mary Pickford lived in the left wing.

### Crossroads of the World
### Sunset Boulevard
### Hollywood

Robert V. Derrah must have spent all of his extra time at the beach. Maybe he just had a great desire to travel the seas. At the same time that he was redesigning the Coca-Cola factory downtown (1936), he was putting together the mad Sunset Boulevard Crossroads of the World. But while the Coca-Cola building is a powerful, almost inhuman statement, the Crossroads is warmly inviting. You're on board a ship sailing past quaint little ports of call. Port, starboard, and aft are small shops styled after harbors the world over.

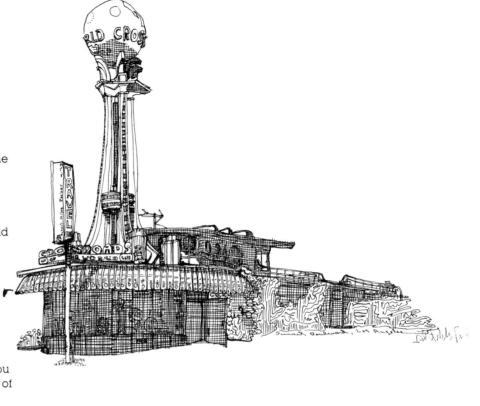

### The Self-Realization Fellowship Center
### 4866 Sunset Boulevard
### Hollywood

The Self-Realization Fellowship Center's architectural style is what you would expect—a hint of India à la Southern California. The designs of golden lotus flowers atop mosque-like pylons suggest the "thousand petaled consciousness center in the brain." The Hollywood center was constructed in 1942. Its architectural style was explicitly based on the teachings of Paramahansa Yogananda, an Indian spiritual leader and the founder of the Self-Realization Fellowship.

## 2020 Beachwood Drive
## Hollywood

Beachwood Drive is the road to Hollywood's beginnings. It leads up to Mount Lee and the Hollywood sign. The sign once said "Hollywoodland," proclaiming a delightful nest of 1920s houses. Hollywoodland still has its charm. But as you follow Beachwood towards town, you pass this deserted house—a sad omen of the Hollywood to come.

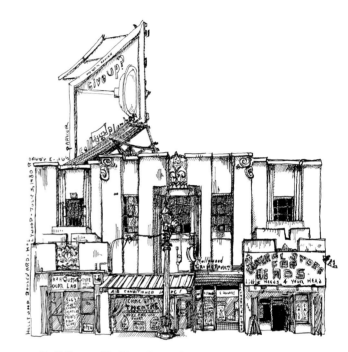

## Building with Plumbing Sign
## 5500 Block of Hollywood Boulevard
## Hollywood

Dr. Hotchkiss across the street (electrotherapy, spinal therapy, and colon irrigation) says he remembers that it was Cecil B. deMille who built this place.

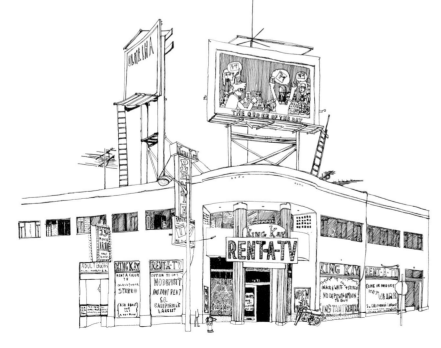

## King Kay Rent-A-TV
## Western Avenue
## Hollywood

Big plate glass windows invite the passing driver to squeal to a halt—those wares are all the more desirable when you see them in grand display. Those are nice Mussolini-esque columns, too.

ROBERT MILES PARKER · JULY 20, 1983                    1840 TAMARIND AVENUE HOLLYWOOD

**The Chateau Elysee** *(left)*
**1840 Tamarind Avenue**
**Hollywood**

Of all the castles that dot Los Angeles, Hollywood's Chateau Elysee is the best. It's strange—none of the major books on L.A.'s architecture discusses this or any of the other castles. Maybe that's okay—castles are better in dreamworlds than in documents.

**1141 and 1143 North Gordon**
**Hollywood**

Looks rather like a fortress, doesn't it? Well, it should. Hollywood's not the glittery fairyland it once was. This Spanish-Moorish design, with its ornamental wooden bars, was meant to evoke pleasant memories of the Old World. But the bars have a functional purpose now. They keep people out.

1141 AND 1143 NORTH GORDON STREET     HOLLYWOOD, CALIFORNIA     ROBERT MILES PARKER MAY, 1982

### The Assyrian Apartments
### 1147 North Gordon
### Hollywood

Somehow this apartment building is not unlike an Assyrian eagle. Or maybe it's an Armenian eagle, reminding the neighbors here of the land of their origin.

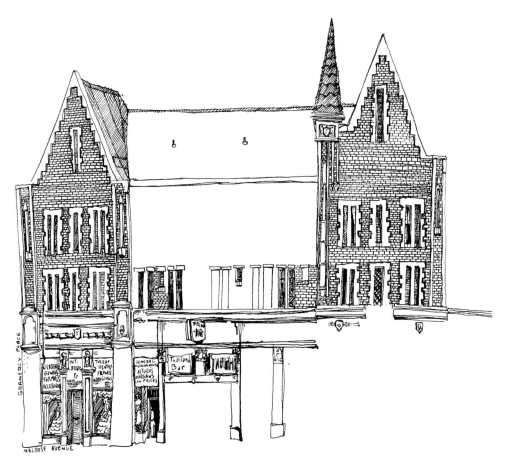

### Tudor Apartment Building
### Melrose Avenue and Gramercy Place
### Hollywood

An English Tudor building. And right down the street may be a Buddhist temple. Nearby, an Egyptian apartment? A Swiss chalet? Just like the film, Hollywood takes you around the world in a very short time.

### The Gauntlet and Herotica
### 8720, 8722 Santa Monica Boulevard
### West Hollywood

West Hollywood is the home of pants stretched tight against muscled thighs on designer bodies strutting Santa Monica Boulevard. Simple stucco houses become the backdrop for a world of pandering.

Herotica proclaims itself as "a sensuality shoppe for women." The Gauntlet sells a slightly different product: body adornments. Ear-piercing and nipple-piercing are the house specialties. And adorned in the wares sold here, the men themselves adorn the boulevard.

### 7700 Block of Santa Monica Boulevard
### West Hollywood

Here we are on Santa Monica Boulevard—pure commercial-strip architecture. And it's pure West Hollywood with its blatantly sexual bazaar. You can also buy the leftover wares of the culture that has been replaced.

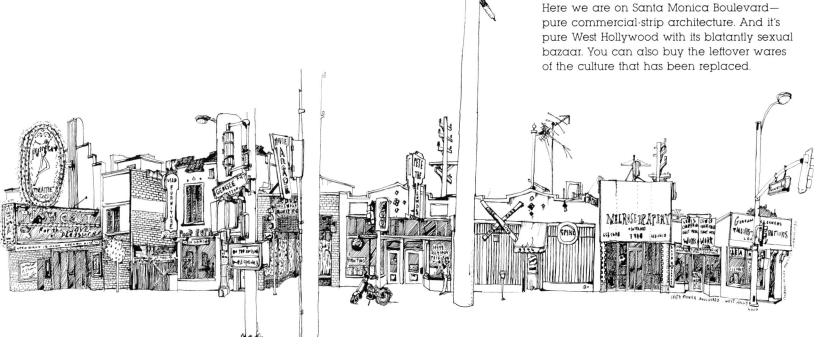

### The Bank of Los Angeles (before)
### 8901 Santa Monica Boulevard
### West Hollywood

The Plant Warehouse was a tired Deco building wilting in the middle of "boys' town." Its salient feature was a tiny fountain-motif tower. That's all been changed now. Where the Plant Warehouse once grew, the Bank of Los Angeles has now sprouted. It is an extremely smart revival of the original Deco structure. It captures the high style that West Hollywood likes to think is its specialty.

This new look was carefully molded by designer Sharon Landa. The Bank of Los Angeles opened in October of 1982. The theme is disco nautical, an update of some of the great Los Angeles buildings. Ms. Landa refers to the style as "postmodern." But its precedessors certainly include buildings like the brash Coca-Cola factory. The ziggurat entryway (shades of the Samson Tyre and Rubber Company) is framed in neon. The neon is carried into the interior spaces, lining walls behind the tellers' cages. But in true West Hollywood style, of course, there are no tellers' cages. Smart young men, and some ladies too, perch behind *Queen Mary* counters.

The Bank of Los Angeles reflects West Hollywood aptly, in aesthetics and in purpose. A major part of its board of directors is gay.

### The Bank of Los Angeles (after)
### 8901 Santa Monica Boulevard
### West Hollywood

**Pacific Design Center** *(right)*
**8687 Melrose Avenue**
**West Hollywood**

New World architecture: glowing blue and spectral. And somehow enticing. "The Blue Whale," as the Design Center is known, is the *very* West Hollywood home for the chic merchants who direct you to the exact chair that will complement Aunt Mildred's old lamp, or to the perfect carpet (violet, like Liz's eyes, of course).

The Center was designed by Cesar Pelli in 1975. It is often described as having charming medieval passageways full of "shops to the trade." But critics have missed the real medieval point of the Whale. It is an impenetrable fortress, excluding the street world. Seen from a distance, the Design Center simply blocks out a hunk of West Hollywood. It's also a bookend, so to speak—Beverly Center to the south completes the matched set. Squeezed in between are very expensive cute shops, very expensive cute homes, and very expensive cute restaurants.

It's an ominous creature, this Design Center, but also beautiful. It bears no architectural relation to West Hollywood, nor to anything else for that matter. But just watch the Blue Whale spawn a new generation of "futuretecture."

**International Male** *(left)*
**9000 Santa Monica Boulevard**
**West Hollywood**

International Male is an L.A. success story—a clothing store that caters to the taste of West Hollywood and the studios. (Though you may not know it, you see International Male fashions all the time on television and in the movies.)

International Male's wardrobes are a continental blend of European and American styles. So is the store's parking lot. It's resplendent with Maseratis and Mercedes—and Fords too. From Rock Hudson to Richard Pryor, they all buy there, and so do the West Hollywood boys. But you'd never know it to look at the dreary, sixties commercial building. That, too, is L.A.

## Tail of the Pup
## 300 North La Cienega
## West Hollywood

The Tail of the Pup's architectural niche is a style called "program-matic," which means the building looks like what it's selling.

On June 10, 1946, *Life* magazine's cover was adorned with a young and pretty Donna Reed. The war was over. And a return to innocence was in the air. The opening of the Tail of the Pup made a photo feature in that same June issue. It's been a Los Angeles tradition ever since.

## Beverly Center
## San Vicente and Beverly Boulevard
## West Hollywood

Beverly Center, like its mate, the Pacific Design Center, is ominous. Its smog-colored bulk fills a whole city block. It denies the cityscape; it is a smug, self-contained giant of a world. On one side, neon escalators zigzag shoppers from street and parking levels, pouring them into interior designer Avner Naggar's very high-tech spaces. The shoppers, too, are high-tech, wearing the latest in smart torn T-shirts and ragged gypsy costumes.

But almost as if in spite of itself, the Center becomes human—at least from this angle. The very popular Hard Rock Cafe, with its fifties Cadillac piercing the roof, invites you in.

Welton Becket and Associates designed Beverly Center and opened the structure in the spring of 1982. It still has a new, unfinished feel. Maybe it's supposed to feel that way always.

## The West Hollywood Pet Hospital
### 127 South San Vicente Boulevard
### West Hollywood

This little building sits right across the street from classy Beverly Center. There it is, squeezed in between two mammoth parking lots, defying the pressures of "unknown parties" who want the land for "other purposes." The West Hollywood Pet Hospital was, by all reports, built in the forties. Dr. Rosenfield came along in 1955. Yes, the building was always this thin—a mere ten feet wide, just like its lot. Rumor has it that Dr. Rosenfield specializes in dachshunds.

## Leftovers on Beverly
### Beverly Boulevard between La Cienega and Huntley
### West Hollywood

A row of folk funk, facing the smart new Beverly Center—on this side, the sleek hulk streaked in neon, and across the way, these shacks. This is architecture that speaks in the vernacular, telling us about the America most of us grew up with. But the Shaggy Uniform Store and Moses' Transfer talk a street lingo that's not long for this upwardly mobile part of the L.A. world.

**Mexican Cottage**
**1201, 1203 Poinsettia Drive**
**West Hollywood**

You couldn't find two cottages more typical of Hollywood's own brand of Mexican heritage. Simple stucco walls, a touch of tile here and there, maybe a niche for an ornament. These buildings and thousands of their siblings retain the quiet charm that delighted their builders and first owners.

ROBERT MILES PARKER · MARCH 4, 1980 · POINTSETTIA DRIVE · WEST HOLLYWOOD

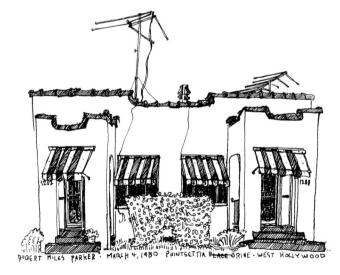

ROBERT MILES PARKER · MARCH 4, 1980 · POINTSETTIA PLACE DRIVE · WEST HOLLYWOOD

**Mexican Cottage**
**1200, 1202 Poinsettia Drive**
**West Hollywood**

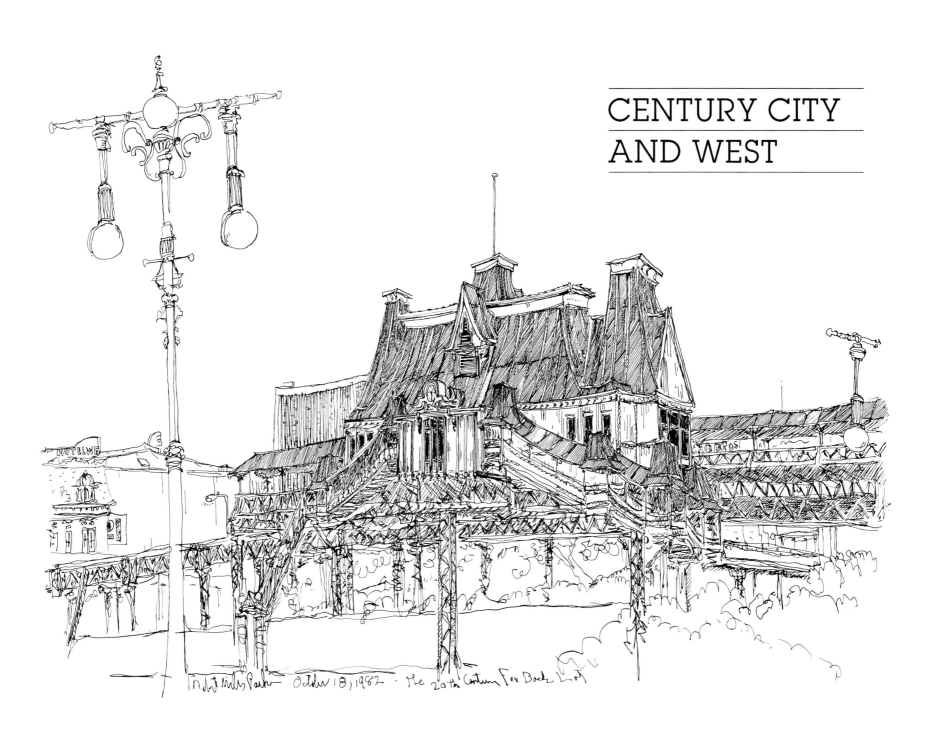

Robert Wills Parker October 18, 1982 - The 20th Century Fox Back Lot

*Hello Dolly* Set, II
Century City

*Hello Dolly* Set, III
Century City

**20th Century Fox Back Lot,**
*Hello Dolly* **Set,** I *(overleaf)*
**Pico and Motor**
**Century City**

The papier-mâché world of cinema comes to
life on Motor Avenue, here on 20th Century
Fox's back lot. These buildings were used in
the musical *Hello Dolly*. They are marvelous
reincarnations of "little ol' New York." And
even with the gleaming, impersonal
skyscrapers of Century City towering in
the background, they command respect.
It's a shame they've been left to fend for
themselves, deteriorating slowly in the hot
sun. The movie industry never has been
famous for taking good care of its own.

**The Witch's House** (*left*)
**Carmelita and Walden**
**Beverly Hills**

Perhaps the perfect symbol for the dream world of Beverly Hills is the Witch's House. Cobwebbed windows, broomsticks, and things that go bump in the night are at home here.

Designed by Harry C. Oliver, the Witch's House was built in 1921. Film buffs may remember that Oliver was art director for *Viva Via*, *The Good Earth*, and *Ben Hur*. He won the first Oscar for design with *Seventh Heaven*. He also invented the cobweb machine.

Mr. Oliver constructed this storybook building as the Irvin Willst Studio. Mr. Willst said about it in April, 1921: "We have tried to reproduce a tumbledown structure of two centuries ago...." The house was originally built in Culver City. Gawkers kept causing traffic accidents, so in 1929, with special dispensation from the city fathers, the structure was moved to its current location. It's lived there happily ever after.

**Natalie Schafer's House** (*right*)
**514 Rodeo Drive**
**Beverly Hills**

The beginnings of Beverly Hills sound just like the beginnings of every other town in the Los Angeles community. The city was originally part of the Rancho Rodeo de las Aguas. It was not until 1906-7 that Burton E. Green created "the Beverly Hills attitude." From the outset, it was the home of, shall we say, successful people. This house is the home of Natalie Schafer, Lovey from "Gilligan's Island."

Here are tree lined streets, manicured parks, Mercedes, and beautiful people. It's an island itself, another Los Angeles fantasy land, a world apart. But Beverly Hills deserves our respect. It is a rather aesthetically successful solution to the need for isolation.

**Hotel Bel Air** (*below*)
**Stone Canyon Road**
**Bel Air**

Bel Air is the most wealthy community in Los Angeles, and the most subtle. A drive through its winding roads is a drive through glorious palms and rich bougainvillea, birds of paradise, elegant eucalyptus—Southern California heaven. This is wealth with a whisper of gentility, echoed on the delicate breeze tickling exotic foliage.

Bel Air was developed by oilman Alphonzo Bell. The Bel Air Hotel (from the mid-forties) was originally his stables. It's a lovely revisitation of Mediterranean architecture, subtle and inviting.

**Hobbit Houses** (*above*)
**3819 Dunn Drive**
**Culver City**

Culver City has more than a touch of architectural fantasy, what with the Witch's House and these absurd Hobbit cottages. Perhaps the reason is that Culver City was an early host to the movie industry—MGM is still there.

The Hobbit houses are a Culver City counterpart to Simon Rodia's Watts Towers. Lawrence Edward Joseph and his wife, Martha, moved to Dunn Drive a year or two after the War. Mr. Joseph has been working on his houses ever since. The furniture and the cabinet work, the floors, even the fixtures—they all have the look of whimsy. Of course, walls curve and floors don't really hold still. And nothing's complete. "No matter. When it's done, it will be done."

JUNCTURE OF
BROXTON AND WESTWOOD
AND KINROSS
WESTWOOD VILLAGE
JULY 26, 1983
ROBERT MILES PARKER

### The Glendale Federal Building
### Junction of Westwood Boulevard, Broxton, and Kinross
### Westwood Village

Smart Westwood Village was developed in the twenties, primarily
by the Janss Development Company, which once occupied this
structure, designed by the firm of Allison and Allison in 1929. From
the outset, the town has maintained a comfortable air. At one time,
Westwood was a lovely ramble of Spanish revival, Monterey revival,
English Norman—all the elegant styles. The Village, too, was a
graceful place. It was laid out as one of America's most successful
suburban shopping centers, planned loosely around a Spanish motif.

The area still has a charm, but it also seems to have more
automobiles than any other community in Los Angeles. Westwood
Village appears to be predominantly streets, with traffic islands full
of light fixtures interspersed with an occasional building. Westwood's
part of Wilshire Boulevard is considered the most heavily traveled
street in the city—a motorized roar of shiny affluence.

It's all clean and well kept, and the inhabitants, a great many
of them young collegiates from UCLA, are as beautiful as the town
once was.

### The Lewis Factor
### Health Sciences Building (below)
### UCLA Campus
### Westwood Village

The Lewis Factor Health Sciences structure
is the tallest building in Westwood Village,
zooming seventeen stories above Westwood
and UCLA. Located on the UCLA campus,
it was designed by Rochlin and Baran
Associates, Los Angeles architects, a firm
specializing in the design of health-care
facilities.

Unlike most tall buildings, this structure
grows broader as it grows up.

## Coin-Op Laundry and Friends
## 11900 Block of Santa Monica Boulevard
## West Los Angeles

West L.A. is definitely the place to live. It's all so nice and middle-class. It's comfortable out there, and clean. (Where else would a laundromat be laundered and hung out to dry?)

## Pancho's Family Dinners
## 12200 Pico Boulevard
## West Los Angeles

Once upon a time, Pancho's was the Round House. At another time it was the Chili Bowl. And at yet another time it was Paco's. This building, whatever its name, is fated to be a family food joint. Nestled on Pico, right by a freeway off-ramp, it's handy for the hungry. And it's as popular a piece of forties programmatic architecture as any in the city.

**View from the Grand Canal** (*overleaf*)
**Venice**

Venice has its origins in a coin flip. Abbot Kinney won that flip in 1904 and got the southern portion of Ocean Park. He had made his fortune with Sweet Corporal cigarettes and used the money to create the town of his dreams: Venice. Most of L.A. is fantasy lands come (partly) true!

Venice became a community with canals and a lagoon. Designed by architects Marsh and Russel, it was to be an elegant place for elegant people. On July 4, 1905, Venice was officially opened. 40,000 people gathered to celebrate "Italy in the West." The Chicago Symphony and Sarah Bernhardt were imported to emphasize the cultural aspects of the new community. It was nice entertainment, but no one bought land. Kinney then brought in amusement rides and sideshows. The more plebeian amusements did the job. Land was sold. Venice came alive. The community became a blend of carny and the arts.

Many of Los Angeles's artists have lived in Venice. There are more murals here than in any other community in L.A. There's also a large Black community in a corner of town called Oakwood, originally the quarter for domestics. The families are still an integral part of Venice life. There is a growing gay population—plus hippies, derelicts, and other strange folk who consider Venice their home. But most of all, Venice is a community of artists.

Venice is wonderful, but it is also mean, with one of the highest crime rates in Los Angeles. Still, people flock to Venice, and it does indeed have a magic. Muscle Beach is still there. So are a few of the original Venice arcade buildings, now dreams gone to decay. But like some dreams, they yield a lingering pleasure. Venice, with its pattern of vacant lots, fortresslike structures, and smart art galleries, is a home for the homeless and a refuge for people who fiercely want to maintain their individuality. Venice structures can be disheveled and perkily trim at the same time.

**Arcade Building** (*right*)
**Windward and Speedway**
**Venice**

ROBERT MILES PARKER · MAY 18, 1983 · WINDWARD AND SPEEDWAY · VENICE

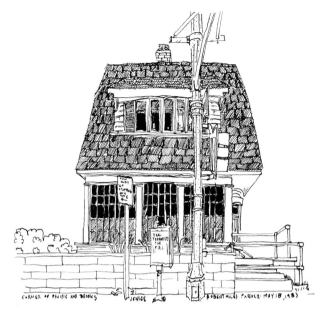

**Martha Alf's House**
**Pacific and Brooks**
**Venice**

**The Getty Museum**
**17985 Pacific Coast Highway**
**Malibu**

J. Paul Getty felt the call to bring back the glories that were Rome and Greece. He wanted to pull together a collection of art called "immortal." He's dead now, but in the film that the museum presents, there he is in his English mansion—his eyes wistful, determined, and bewildered and his lower lip trembling—talking about immortality and his collection and his museum.

The museum is filled with Greek pottery and French painting and decorative art. It opened in 1974. Mr. Getty died in 1976, but he never saw his museum.

The most important piece in this recreated Roman villa is Lysippos' bronze of an athlete. The young man is alive, breathing. He has just raised his arm and has paused. And you, the viewer, stop breathing. That's immortality.

## Santa Monica Pier
## Santa Monica

The Santa Monica Pier was constructed around the time of the First World War, and though it's now only a remnant of its former self, it still sings the rinky-tink song an ocean pier should.

Santa Monica, the city, is a determined maverick, the Peck's bad boy of L.A. It has retained more individuality than most Los Angeles communities. Unfortunately, it did succumb to the ravages of Ernest Hahn. As in Pasadena, Mr. Hahn slapped a shopping center in the middle of downtown, which thumbs its nose at the architectural integrity of Santa Monica's commercial area.

The town was originally ranch land, until Senator John P. Jones of Nevada went into partnership with Colonel Robert S. Baker, the owner of the ranch, to create what they hoped would be a great port metropolis. Town plans were filed in 1875, and lots of people came to Santa Monica. Despite the decision to make San Pedro the port of L.A., Santa Monica survived. And flourished.

Santa Monica struggles to keep an atmosphere of its own. The Pier is still there—at least part of it is. Enveloping the rambling structure is the smell of corn dogs in competition with salty ocean breezes. Young lovers stroll hand in hand, and local toughs impress their girls at the shooting gallery.

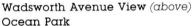

**Wadsworth Avenue View** (*above*)
**Ocean Park**

Ocean Park is the southernmost part of Santa Monica—just above Venice. Its late Victorian homes are proudly maintained as a reminder of ocean-side living in a more genteel time.

**Fort MacArthur and the Patton Quadrangle** (*right*)
**San Pedro**

The Fort MacArthur area was mentioned by Cabrillo as early as 1542. Declared a military reservation by Grover Cleveland in 1888, the area has since been made part of America's defense system.

Fort MacArthur is the site of the Casa de San Pedro hide house, the first commercial structure on the shore of San Pedro Bay. It was built in 1823 by the trading firm of McCullogh and Hartnell and was designed to store cattle hides from the San Gabriel and San Fernando Missions. And so began the development of the port of Los Angeles.

Tranquil Patton Quadrangle is named in honor of old "Blood and Guts" Patton. The General was born in San Gabriel, and his father was a D.A. for Los Angeles County. The windy quadrangle buildings were constructed between 1917 and 1919, and restoration began in 1982. The quadrangle suggests a time when war was a more gentlemanly pursuit.

**San Pedro Queen Anne** (*above*)
**329 10th Street**
**San Pedro**

San Pedro has a ramshackle, East-coast feeling about it. It was an independent city until 1909, when it was made part of Los Angeles. As early as the 1850s, the town was being mentioned as a port city. The first harbor improvements were made in 1887, and in 1892 efforts to make San Pedro a deep-water port began. L.A. finally got its link to the sea.

Vestiges of the original town, such as this charming Queen Anne Victorian, are not hard to find. It's fun to wander the streets, searching out San Pedro's hidden jewels.

**The USS *Berkeley*
Naval Shipyard
Long Beach**

The Long Beach Naval Shipyard was established at Terminal Island in 1940. The first ship was dry-docked there in 1942. The area is a confusion of cranes and ships, a beehive of workers. The shipyard is one of the three largest industries in the city of Long Beach. Within an area of 214 acres, there are three graving docks, five industrial piers, and "Herman the German." (He's a prize from World War II and one of the three largest cranes in existence.)

The USS *Berkeley* visited the shipyard in April of 1983. It's a classic, twenty-year-old destroyer. The ship berths 350 men, most of them disarmingly young and sincere. The *Berkeley* herself exudes sincerity. Her men treat her with pride, and she deserves it.

Los Angeles is constant host to ships like the *Berkeley*, machines most of us never think about, which protect us out beyond our horizons.

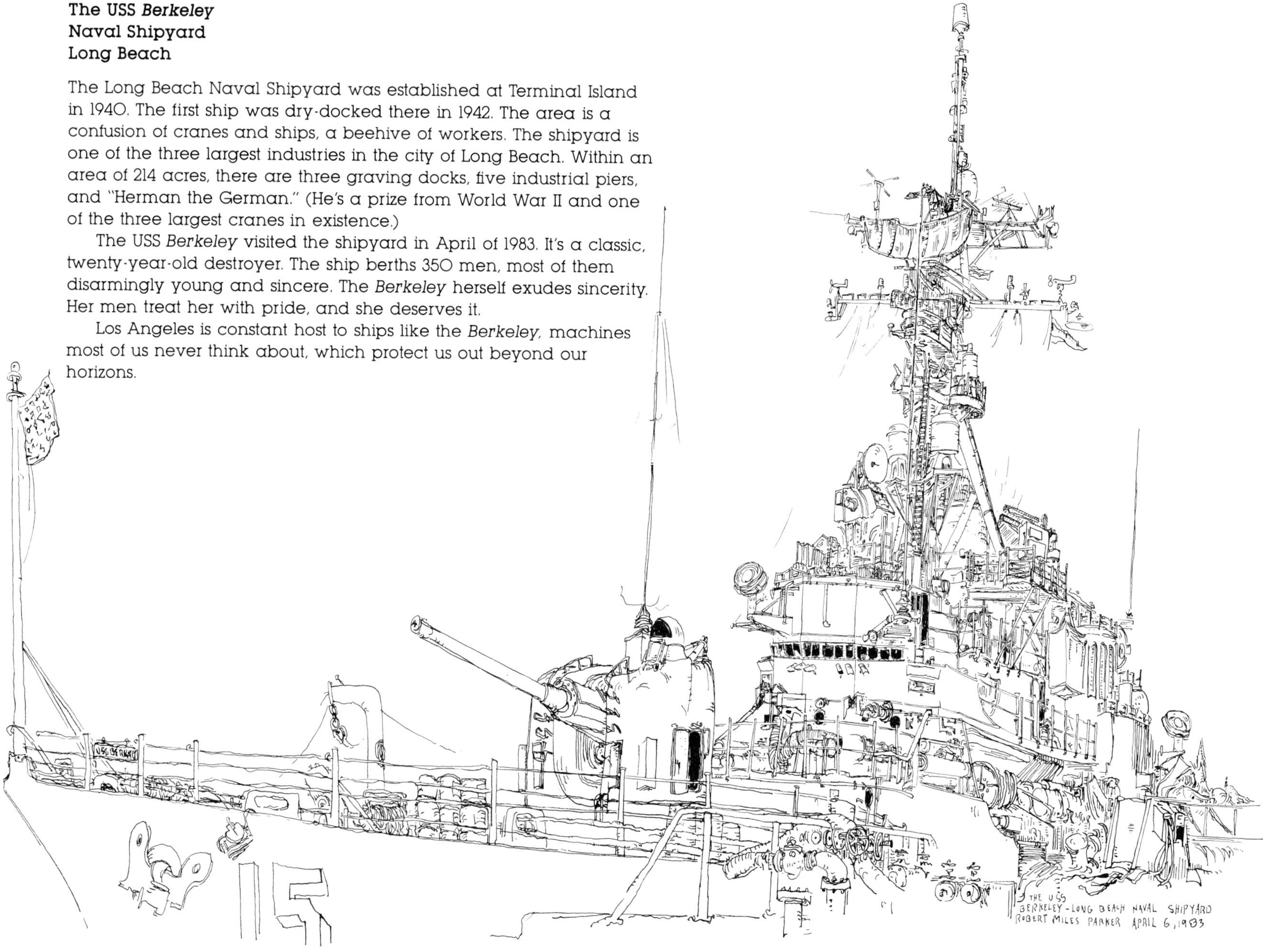

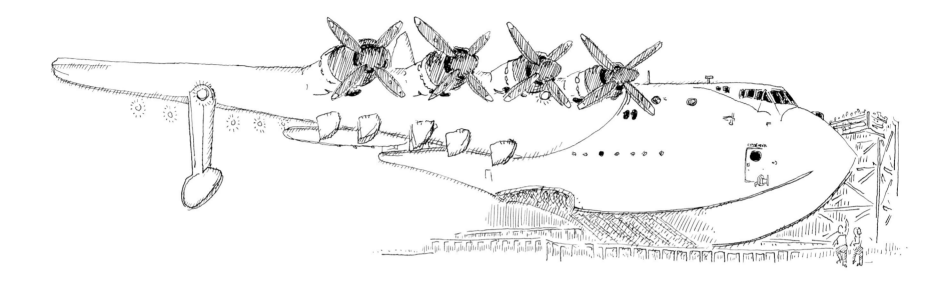

**The Spruce Goose**
**Long Beach Pier**
**Long Beach**

The Spruce Goose is beautiful, even if it does have a silly name.
It is almost incomprehensibly huge and sleek.

Howard Hughes designed the airplane, which has been flown
only once and for only a few minutes. After 1947, the plane was
hidden away. But now it is another Los Angeles entertainment star,
resting in the world's largest free-standing dome. The plane was
designed to be a troop and provision carrier. It can hold up to 750
troops or a sixty-ton Sherman tank. The Goose is 219 feet long, its tail is
eight stories high, and, as the billboards say, a DC 10 can be parked
under each wing.

The dome itself is a glorious complement to Mr. Hughes's airplane.
A resplendent light show offers colors varying from bright yellow
daylight to the soft blue of evening. The Spruce Goose basks in the
gentle aura created for it. Tourists, however, have been known to
grumble at the light show. While mothers nag at fussing children,
disheveled fathers struggle vainly to adjust their light meters to the
shifting colors.

**The Queen Mary**
**Long Beach Pier**
**Long Beach**

It's somehow appropriate that Britain's fastest (and most luxurious) ship, the Queen Mary, has been permanently berthed in Los Angeles. No doubt it was L.A.'s preoccupation with all things nautical that compelled it to search out and honor this particular immigrant. From the Shrimp House out in Claremont to the Coca-Cola Bottling Company downtown, from the Crossroads of the World on Sunset Boulevard to the Ocean Seafood Restaurant in Alhambra—Los Angeles's nautical obsession demanded a grand architectural culmination.

The Queen Mary, commissioned in 1926 by the Cunard Steamship Company, took her maiden voyage in 1936. She came to rest in Los Angeles in December of 1967. The City of Angels added one more star to its heavens, a polestar for its continuing journey.

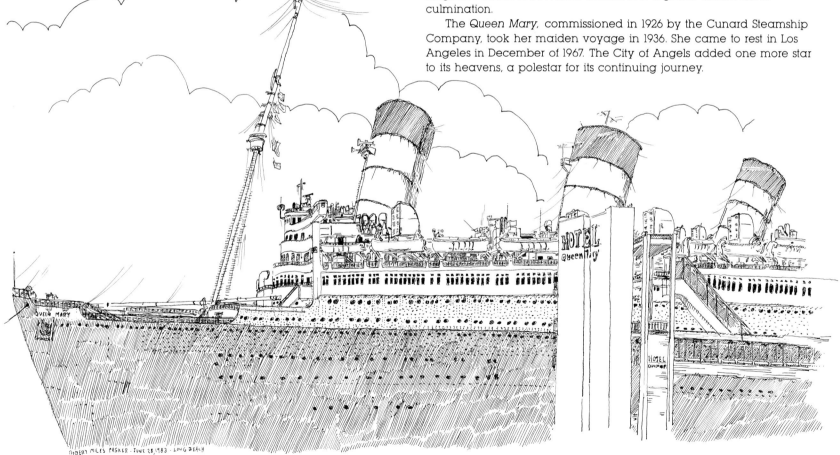

ROBERT MILES PARKER · JUNE 28, 1983 · LONG BEACH

5826 Olympic Boulevard at Curson

# THE DRAWINGS

# THE COLLECTORS

View from Welcome Street
Patricia Schachlin
La Jolla, California

View into Downtown
Patricia Clark
Falls Church, Virginia

The Downtown Library
Dr. and Mrs. Donald Mitchell
San Diego, California

The Oviatt Building
Nancy and Graham McHutchin
La Jolla, California

The *Times* Building
Dr. Robert Nevlin and Amy Nevlin
San Diego, California

The Coca-Cola Bottling Company
Marc Tarasuck
San Diego, California

St. Vincent Court
Hillary and Richard Sanderson
Pasadena, California

The Maplewood
David Lange
San Diego, California

1126 Mignonette Street
Bert Waxler
San Diego, California

Old Victorian
Cathy and Ron Rees
San Diego, California

The First AME Church
Mrs. Edna Tolbert
Pasadena, California

The Bonnie Brae Apartments
Rich Romo
San Diego, California

Alvarado Street and Maryland Street
Rich Romo
San Diego, California

The Bonnie Brae House
Harry Evans
San Diego, California

The Pellissier Building and Wiltern Theater
Kenneth M. Arellanez
La Mesa, California

The Bella Vista Apartments and Shops
John Woods
San Diego, California

Bullock's Wilshire
Scott Brown and Robert Kinsell
San Diego, California

The Brown Derby
Nickie Chaisson
San Diego, California

The Old Tom Bergin's
Deborah Warren
Cardiff, California

St. Andrews Place
Peter De Luca
Los Angeles, California

The Mutual of Omaha Building
Terry J. Horton
North Hollywood, California

Park La Brea
John Chamberlin
Tucson, Arizona

Meaty Meat Burgers
Gary Rees
San Diego, California

Fairfax
Patricia Clark
Falls Church, Virginia

The Pan Pacific Building
Fred Acheson
San Diego, California

Randy's Donuts
Linda Bonham
San Diego, California

The Gill Railway Station
Bruce Kamerling
San Diego, California

The Tamale
David L. Bratton
Santee, California

County General Hospital
Dr. Gary Lee Dugan
Castro Valley, California

The Church of Christian Hope
Dan Creasy
San Diego, California

Lincoln Hospital
Dr. Chip Bogosian
Seattle, Washington

The Cummings Block
Jim Shaver
Pacific Palisades, California

Chinatown View
Ken McNames and Michael Duddy
Houston, Texas

The Goldberg House
Dr. and Mrs. Herb Goldberg
Los Angeles, California

View from Echo Park Avenue
James A. Hyndman
San Diego, California

Angelus Temple
Rev. Robert Northrop
San Diego, California

The Ennis-Brown House
Phil Derkum
Denver, Colorado

Shakespeare Bridge View
Dr. George Mahan
San Diego, California

The Griffith Observatory
R.K. Benites
San Diego, California

Disneyland
Carole and David Fluke
Nevada City, California

Knott's Berry Farm—Ghost Town:
   Goldie's Place
Bertie Lovell
San Diego, California

Pat Diamond's House
Pat Diamond
Fullerton, California

The 302 Cafe, the La Gloria,
   and the West Coast Theater
Lilly Rosa Hansmann and Gary Hansmann
San Diego, California

The Antioch Baptist Church
Karen Johls
San Diego, California

The Stevens House
Carmen Cunningham Williams
Paris, France

The Castle Green
Betty Peterson
San Diego, California

The Donut Hole
Mr. and Mrs. Mark Braverman
San Diego, California

The Santa Anita Race Track
Ruth McMichael
Leucadia, California

The Huntington Library
Karen and Abner Hunt
San Diego, California

Andrianna's View
Andre Jovan and Penny Valliere
Claremont, California

Le Chateau
Dale Craig
San Diego, California

Bullock's Pasadena
Joey Muna
New York, New York

The Rose Bowl
Cathy DeFino
San Diego, California

Gary's View of North Hollywood
Nicole and Gary Peterson
North Hollywood, California

The Edmund House
Monica Edmund
San Francisco, California

The Warner Brothers Building
Penny Ann Pergament
San Diego, California

Our Lady of Peace Church
Paul-Kip Otis Diehl
Newport, Rhode Island

Hollywood Tower
Gwen Snyder
San Diego, California

J. J. Newberry
Devora and Tommy Bratton
La Honda, California

Frederick's of Hollywood
Ellen Tyson
San Diego, California

The Garden Court Apartment Hotel
Paul Scott
Louisville, Kentucky

Mann's Chinese Theater
Paul McNalley
Hollywood, California

Paramount Studios—South Gate
John Evertse
La Mesa, California

The Trianon
Merika Adams Gopaul
San Diego, California

Deco Building on Santa Monica
Max Springer
San Diego, California

Crossroads of the World
Merika Adams Gopaul
San Diego, California

2020 Beachwood Drive
Pat Hyndman
La Mesa, California

The Chateau Elysee
Betsy Gates
San Diego, California

The Gauntlet and Herotica
Mark Gomez
National City, California

International Male
Gene Burkhard
San Diego, California

Tail of the Pup
Carleton Knight III
Washington, D.C.

Beverly Center
Jeff McGreevy
San Diego, California

Mexican Cottage
Reuben Schneider
San Diego, California

Mexican Cottage
Mr. and Mrs. Philip Levin
West Hollywood, California

20th Century Fox Back Lot, *Hello Dolly* Set, I
Helen E. Bratton
Santee, California

*Hello Dolly* Set, II
Dale Craig and John Homeburg
San Diego, California

The Witch's House
Nancy Hayward
Encinitas, California

The Lewis Factor Health Sciences Building
Rochlin and Baran Associates
Los Angeles, California

Pancho's Family Dinners
Danielle and Rick Ybarra
San Diego, California

View from the Grand Canal
Stephen Brixner
San Diego, California

The Getty Museum
Suann Amber Dawn
Casa de Oro, California

Santa Monica Pier
Dorothy and David Pascoe
El Cajon, California

Wadsworth Avenue View
Douglas Scot Lenhart
San Diego, California

The USS *Berkeley*
Cmdr. and Mrs. Robin Reighley
San Diego, California

The Spruce Goose
Dr. Chip Bogosian
Seattle, Washington

The Queen *Mary*
Dr. and Mrs. Harvey Lobelson
San Diego, California

5826 Olympic Boulevard at Curson
Terry Horton
North Hollywood, California